W9-AUY-410

NORTH KOREA

ABDO
Publishing Company

NORTH KOREA

by Racquel Foran

Content Consultant
Balbina Hwang
Visiting Professor, Georgetown University

CREDITS

Published by ABDO Publishing Company, PO Box 398166, Minneapolis, MN 55439.
Copyright © 2013 by Abdo Consulting Group, Inc. International copyrights reserved
in all countries. No part of this book may be reproduced in any form without written
permission from the publisher. The Essential Library™ is a trademark and logo of ABDO
Publishing Company.

Printed in the United States of America,
North Mankato, Minnesota
092012
012013

♻ THIS BOOK CONTAINS AT LEAST 10% RECYCLED MATERIALS.

Editor: Arnold Ringstad
Series Designer: Emily Love

About the Author: Racquel Foran is a freelance writer living in Coquitlam, British
Columbia, Canada. She enjoys writing about politics, current events, and social issues and
is a frequent contributor to magazines and newspapers in her region.

Cataloging-in-Publication Data

Foran, Racquel.
 North Korea / Racquel Foran.
   p. cm. -- (Countries of the world)
Includes bibliographical references and index.
ISBN 978-1-61783-632-9
1. Korea (North)--Juvenile literature.   I. Title.
951.93--dc22

2012946073

Cover: The Grand People's Study House in Pyongyang

TABLE OF CONTENTS

CHAPTER 1	A Visit to North Korea	6
	Map: Political Boundaries of North Korea	9
	Snapshot	17
CHAPTER 2	Geography: Mountains, Valleys, and Seas	18
	Map: Geography of North Korea	22
	Map: Climate of North Korea	26
CHAPTER 3	Animals and Nature: The Accidental Preserve	30
CHAPTER 4	History: A Land of Conflict	42
CHAPTER 5	People: Watched and Controlled	60
	Map: Population Density of North Korea	65
CHAPTER 6	Culture: A Single Theme	70
CHAPTER 7	Politics: One Man, No Votes	86
CHAPTER 8	Economics: A Faltering System	100
	Map: Resources of North Korea	111
CHAPTER 9	North Korea Today	114
TIMELINE		128
FACTS AT YOUR FINGERTIPS		130
GLOSSARY		134
ADDITIONAL RESOURCES		136
SOURCE NOTES		138
INDEX		142
PHOTO CREDITS		144

CHAPTER 1

A VISIT TO NORTH KOREA

As your plane touches down at Pyongyang's Sunan International Airport, you get your first peek of North Korea through the window. To your surprise, you don't see much of anything. It is normal to feel apprehensive, as North Korea is one of the most closed, isolated, and mysterious countries in the world today. Despite having arrived at the country's largest and only international airport, the runway is empty. Americans are rarely allowed entry and the government is secretive, so you know little about the nation and its people, but you are curious. What are the people really like? What do they know about the rest of the world? How do they spend their time? What kind of music and art do they like? You hope your visit to North Korea—also

All foreign visitors to North Korea must be hosted by a local organization.

The streets of Pyongyang are quiet even in the middle of the day.

known as the Democratic People's Republic of Korea (DPRK)—will answer some of these questions.

Cell phones are not permitted in North Korea, so after handing yours over to officials to be retrieved upon your departure, you collect your luggage and head for the exit. You know foreigners are not allowed to travel freely around the country without a guide, and taxis and other forms of transportation cannot be found at the airport, so you are relieved to find a representative from your host organization already waiting for you when you step outside. Before leaving, you turn to take a picture of the airport, but your guide quickly advises you that taking photos of any government or military facilities is forbidden.

As your guide navigates his old Mercedes through the streets of Pyongyang, you take in your surroundings and are once

SUNAN INTERNATIONAL AIRPORT

Located 15 miles (24 km) north of the capital city, Sunan International Airport is the only international airport in the country; almost all foreign visitors arrive and depart from this airport. In addition to Air Koryo, North Korea's national airline, Air China and Vladivostok Air also provide flights in and out of the country. There are three weekly flights serving Beijing, as well as weekly connections to Shenyang in northeast China and Vladivostok in eastern Russia. There are also occasional flights to Shanghai, China. Although it is an international airport, Pyongyang only handles between 15 and 20 flights a week; this number has increased in recent years from as few as five flights a week in 2006.

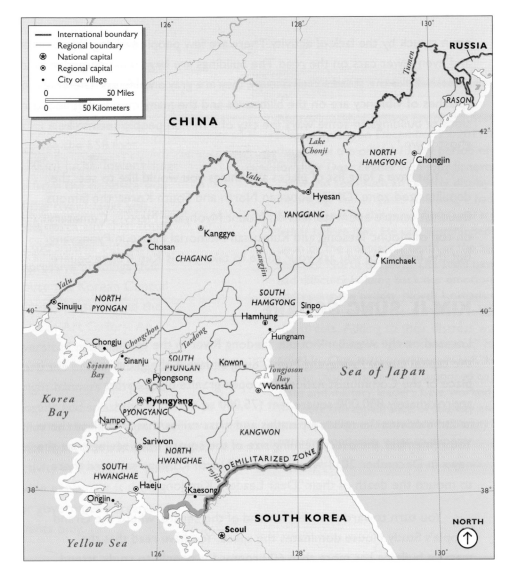

Political Boundaries of North Korea

Kim Il Sung Square sits on the banks of the Taedong River.

You are beginning to realize that learning more about this isolated country and its people's everyday activities is going to be difficult—it is not only foreigners' movements and communications that are restricted. Even locals are monitored and controlled.

It wasn't always this way. For almost 60 years, since the division of the Korean Peninsula, North Korea has been run by a totalitarian Communist dictatorship. Kim Il Sung took power in 1948 and held power until his death in 1994. He is known in North Korea as the "Great Leader," and the nation's constitution declares him to be the "Eternal President." His son Kim Jong Il succeeded him, ruling until his own death in 2011. Kim Jong Il was often referred to as the "Dear Leader." Since then, Kim Jong Il's son Kim Jong Un has been the country's supreme leader. Though North Korea's official name is the Democratic

COMMUNISM

Karl Marx, a nineteenth-century German philosopher whose writings formed the foundation for communism, believed the fall of capitalism was inevitable and that communism would replace it. He theorized there were two stages in this process. First was a temporary period when the working class would control the government but essentially run it the same way it had been. The final stage was a complete Communist state, where there would be no class divisions. The first phase is what most now consider socialism; the second is the ideal of communism. Unfortunately, as socialism gained popularity throughout the twentieth century, the ruling Communist governments leaned towards totalitarian dictatorships, and true equality among the people in Communist states was never really accomplished. At its height, communism was practiced by approximately one third of the world's governments.

By 2012, there were only five Communist countries left: China, Cuba, Laos, Vietnam, and North Korea. All except North Korea have opened their borders to more trade, even while dictatorships have remained. North Korea is unlike other Communist nations in that power is handed down from father to son.

People's Republic of Korea, in practice there is little democracy to be found.

The government controls all aspects of citizens' lives. All media outlets, including radio, television, and newspapers, are owned by the government. Internet access is also restricted and monitored. Only a few thousand foreigners are granted entry to the country each year, and even locals are not always allowed to travel from the countryside to the city without a permit. The government tightly controls the economy, influences which jobs people take, and rations food.

International drivers' licenses are not accepted in North Korea.

HOMOGENOUS SOCIETY

North Korea is one of the most culturally, ethnically, and racially homogenous countries in the world. Our modern ability to travel the globe and communicate easily with people thousands of miles away means there are few countries that have not been influenced by cross-cultural exposure and interracial marriages, but North Korea is one of them.

After the Korean War (1950–1953), North Korea's leader Kim Il Sung essentially cut the country off from the rest of the world, ensuring that outsiders and especially South Korea could not influence the North

North Korean people relax in Pyongyang. Citizens have little or no contact with the world outside their country.

Korean people. He then proceeded to demonize the United States by rewriting history; North Koreans have been told falsely that their nation defeated Japan in World War II (1937–1945) and that the United States started the Korean War.

In addition to changing history to suit his politics, Kim Il Sung also closed the borders, restricted travel, and limited communications. At the same time, he used government funds to spread propaganda promoting his Juche ideology. Juche emphasizes Korean nationalism and self-reliance. He also encouraged the belief that the Korean Peninsula would one day be reunited under his family's rule. The result is a citizenship that looks and acts almost uniformly alike. Virtually all of the population is 100 percent Korean. The majority of the people claim no religious affiliation. Celebrations are massive staged events that involve many thousands of people. Even when they mourn as they did when their leader died, they do so in an orchestrated public display. The government controls what North Koreans read and learn. Visitors' interviews with citizens are monitored and restricted; it is difficult to know how many citizens, if any, question what they are told.

The large banner hanging above Kim Il Sung Square carries a slogan that can be found in many other places around the country: "We have nothing to envy in the world."[6] The leaders of North Korea may convince their citizens of this, but after your visit, will you believe it yourself?

SNAPSHOT

Official name: Democratic People's Republic of Korea (DPRK)

Capital city: Pyongyang

Form of government: Communist dictatorship

Titles of leaders: supreme leader (dictator); president (chief of state); premier (head of government)

Currency: North Korean won

Population (July 2012 est.): 24,589,122
World rank: 49

Size: 46,540 square miles (120,538 sq km)
World rank: 99

Language: Korean

Official religion: none; religious activities are largely nonexistent, and government-sponsored religious groups give the illusion of religious freedom. The country was traditionally Buddhist and Confucianist, with some Christian adherents.

Per capita GDP (2011, US dollars): $1,800
World rank: 193

CHAPTER 2

CHAPTER 2

GEOGRAPHY AND CLIMATE: MOUNTAINS, VALLEYS, AND SEAS

North Korea is a country dominated by peaks and valleys. Jutting 620 miles (998 km) southward from the northeast section of the Asian continent, the Korean Peninsula features dramatic mountain ranges cascading into the Sea of Japan to the east and a collection of islands and coves scattered about the Yellow Sea to the west.[1]

LOCATION

North Korea is located in eastern Asia and occupies the northern half of the Korean Peninsula. It covers 46,540 square miles (120,538 sq km), accounting for 55 percent of the peninsula. The country is slightly

The Yalu River and North Korea as seen from the Chinese border

PROPAGANDA IN THE HILLS

Propaganda can be seen all over North Korea, even outside the cities and deep in the countryside. Propaganda signs are often the only splashes of color in an otherwise dull landscape. Even gray granite mountainsides have been emblazoned with slogans promoting the Communist way of life. The massive red lettering always appears freshly painted. Phrases like "Long live Kim Il Sung," "Let's live our own way," and "We will do as the party tells us" mark the landscape.

smaller than the state of Mississippi.[2] North Korea shares two borders to the north: one with China that is 885 miles (1,425 km) long, and a much smaller 12-mile (19 km) one with Russia. The Yalu River, which runs southwest, and the Tumen River, which runs northeast, create a natural border between North Korea and its northern neighbors. South Korea occupies the southern half of the peninsula; a demilitarized zone separates the two countries along the 38th parallel. This is the line at 38° north latitude.

The nation is divided into nine provinces and two municipalities. The capital city Pyongyang, located in the municipality of the same name, is in the central-west part of the country.

SEAS AND MOUNTAINS

The Korea Bay and Yellow Sea lie to the west, and the Sea of Japan (also known as the East Sea) lies to the east. The two coastlines are very different. Most of the high mountain ranges can be found in the east, where they drop steeply into the 6,000-foot (1,800 m) deep Sea of Japan.[3] In contrast, the west coast slopes more gradually into the 160-foot (50 m) deep Korea Bay.[4] The bay is also full of small islands and coves. Less than half of the peninsula's 5,256 miles (8,460 km) of coastlines are within North Korea's borders, and the people rely heavily on these areas for food.[5] Much of North Koreans' protein comes from fishing in the seas that surround them.

North Korea's landscape is dominated by mountains and highlands. Mountain ranges crisscross the country, making most of the land unsuitable for development or agriculture.

MOUNT PAEKTU

Mount Paektu, which sits on the border between China and North Korea, has long been considered a sacred place by both North and South Korea. Mount Paektu is a breathtaking location. Deep within the crater of the extinct volcano, a lake has formed. Lake Chonji is one of the deepest alpine lakes in the world; it is easy to see why this location became a place of legend. Early Korean legend has it that Lake Chonji is the site where the god Hwanung descended from the heavens to the earth to form a divine city.

Following World War II, the Kim family propaganda machine changed the mountain's meaning. According to this new history, it is at the base of Mount Paektu that Kim Il Sung bravely fought a Japanese army 1 million strong. North Korean history books claim that with godlike powers Kim Il Sung annihilated the Japanese. And, despite records indicating he was born in Russia, this is also where Kim Il Sung claimed his son Kim Jong Il was born; it was important that the heir to the Communist dictator be born on Korean soil. Kim Jong Il's invented birthplace in a guerrilla camp on the face of Mount Paektu is now a place of pilgrimage and worship for North Koreans.

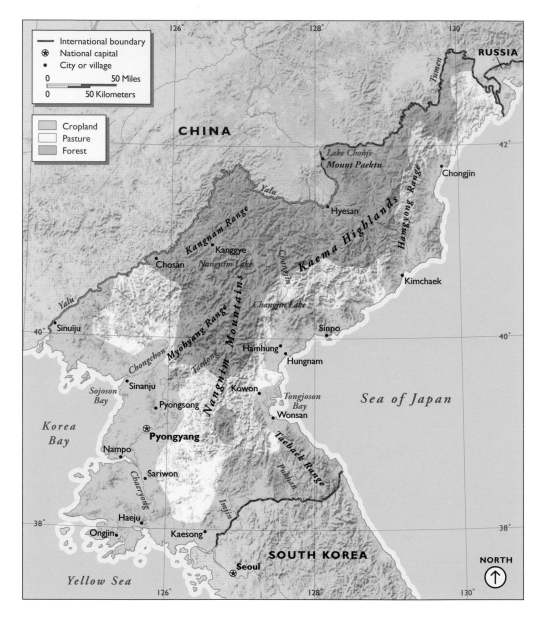

International boundary
⊛ **National capital**
• **City or village**

0   50 Miles
0   50 Kilometers

Cropland
Pasture
Forest

CHINA

RUSSIA

Tumen

Lake Chonji
Mount Paektu

• Chongjin

Yalu

• Hyesan

Kangnam Range

• Kanggye

Hamgyong Range

• Chosan

Nangrim Lake

Kaema Highlands

Changjin

• Kimchaek

Changjin Lake

Yalu

• Sinuiju

Myohyang Range

• Sinpo

Nangnim Mountains

• Hamhung

Chongchon

• Hungnam

Taedong

• Sinanju

Sojoson
Bay

• Kowon

Tongjoson
Bay

Sea of Japan

• Pyongsong

• Wonsan

Korea
Bay

⊛ **Pyongyang**

• Nampo

Taebaek Range

• Sariwon

Chaeryong

Pukhan

Imjin

• Haeju

• Ongjin

• Kaesong

SOUTH KOREA

NORTH
↑

Yellow Sea

⊛ **Seoul**

Geography of North Korea

The Nangnim Mountains are located in the north-central part of North Korea and run north to south, essentially splitting the country into western and eastern halves. This geographical divide makes it very difficult for people to travel from one side of the country to the other. Extending west from this range are the Kangnam and the Myohyang Ranges, which run parallel to each other along the North Korea–China border. The Taebaek Range runs along the east coast from southeastern North Korea into South Korea.

The Kaema Highlands run through the extreme northeastern part of the peninsula. With an average elevation of 3,300 feet (1,006 m) above sea level, the plateau is known as the "roof of the Korean Peninsula."[6] This is where you will find Mount Paektu; at 9,003 feet (2,744 m), it is thousands of feet higher than the mountain ranges that surround it.[7] An extinct volcano with a lake in its crater, Paektu has long held strong spiritual symbolism for the Korean people.

RIVERS AND VALLEYS

Rushing down from the mountaintops is a network of rivers that run westward to the Korea Bay. The Chongchon, Chaeryong, Taedong, and Yalu Rivers all flow to the west coast; only one river, the Tumen, drains into the Sea of Japan on the east coast. Although the country has almost 1,400 miles (2,250 km) of inland waterways, most are navigable only by small boats.[8] The Yalu, Tumen, and Taedong are the most navigable and therefore most important waterways in North Korea.

Vast plains with rich soil stretch across many of the narrow western river valleys, forming large agricultural regions throughout the area. Most of the country's population lives in these fertile lowlands as well as in small pockets along the coastal plains of the east coast. The largest plains are the Pyongyang and Chaeryong.

PREPARING FOR AN ERUPTION

After a devastating earthquake and tsunami struck Japan in 2011, South Korea and North Korea got together for a rare consultation to discuss the possible impacts of an eruption of Mount Paektu. It has long been believed that the volcano is extinct, but recent satellite images indicate it might actually have an active core. An eruption would be catastrophic, potentially causing Lake Chonji to overflow and flood the area. Thirteen North Koreans, including several volcano specialists, met with four South Korean geologists for a day of talks on the matter.

CLIMATE

North Korea experiences seasons at the same time of year as North America. The climate is generally temperate, with most rain coming in the summer months. Because of humid summer monsoons in the Pacific Ocean, three-fifths of the yearly rainfall occurs between June and September; typhoons occasionally occur in these months. In August 2011, a

A crater lake fills the top of Mount Paektu.

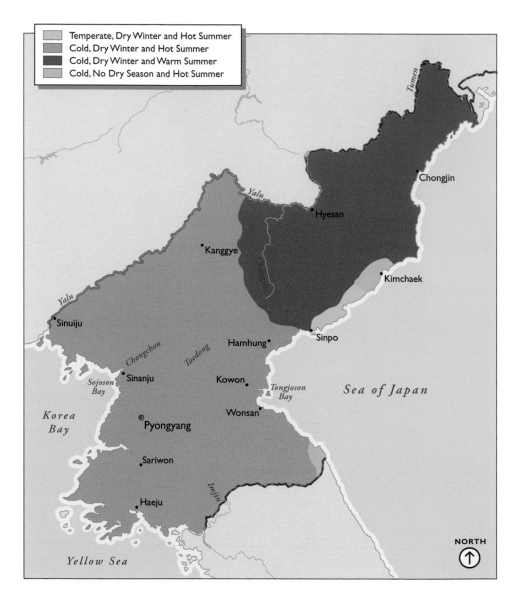

Temperate, Dry Winter and Hot Summer
Cold, Dry Winter and Hot Summer
Cold, Dry Winter and Warm Summer
Cold, No Dry Season and Hot Summer

Climate of North Korea

AVERAGE TEMPERATURE AND PRECIPITATION

Region (City)	Average January Temperature Minimum/Maximum	Average July Temperature Minimum/Maximum	Average Precipitation January/July
Pyongyang Plain (Pyongyang)	14/29°F (-10/-1°C)	69/82°F (20/27°C)	0.6/9.9 inches (1/25 cm)
East Coast (Wonsan)	22/34°F (-5/1°C)	68/77°F (20/25°C)	1.4/15.5 inches (3/39 cm)
West Coast (Haeju)	20/32°F (-6/0°C)	70/79°F (21/26°C)	0.7/18.8 inches (1/47 cm)[10]

typhoon struck the Korean Peninsula, killing four South Koreans and ten North Koreans.

Winters are cold, with temperatures dipping below -10°F (-23°C) in the interior north.[9] All areas can get snow, but the heaviest snowfalls usually occur high in the mountains. Many prefer to visit North Korea in either the spring or fall, when rainfall is light and the temperatures are comfortable.

North Korea has told its citizens to use pets as early warning systems for earthquakes.

THE CITIES

Both the geography and climate of North Korea influence where people live. Many areas of the country are uninhabitable because of severe weather, rugged terrain, or both. Traveling from one side of the country to another is not easy; there is no extensive road system to support travel between cities. The central government strictly restricts the movement of citizens between cities, and one must receive permission to travel outside of one's designated home region.

Only 22 percent of North Korea's land is arable.

There are, however, a number of relatively large cities scattered across the country: Rason and Chongjin in the North Hamgyong province; Hamhung in the South Hamgyong province; the capital Pyongyang; and Sinuiju in the North Pyongan province. The growth of many of these cities can be attributed to their proximity to North Korea's borders and coastlines.

Pyongyang is North Korea's largest city.

CHAPTER 3

ANIMALS AND NATURE: THE ACCIDENTAL PRESERVE

Amur leopards, Asiatic bears, antelope, and raccoon dogs are among the dozens of species of animals that roam the northern part of the Korean Peninsula. The extremely rare Siberian tiger, sometimes spotted here, is considered by some to be a national animal of North Korea. But years of war and deforestation have led to a decline of these and many other species. Migratory waterfowl, cranes, and herons still populate the plains, but the wealth of animal diversity is now concentrated in the demilitarized zone (DMZ).

Part of the canine family, the raccoon dog looks like a cross between a fox and a raccoon.

Though they are rare, Siberian tigers have been known to live in North Korea.

ASIATIC BLACK BEAR

The Asiatic black bear is very similar in size and shape to its American black bear cousin. Its relatively large ears and the unique white crescent-shaped patch on its chest differentiate it. It once roamed vast areas of Southeast and East Asia from Afghanistan to Japan. Now it is listed as a vulnerable species. The bears are found mostly in remote areas of China, Russia, and North Korea. The main reason for their dwindling numbers—other than deforestation—is poaching. Thousands of bears are killed for their gall bladders every year; modern practitioners of traditional Chinese medicine believe bear gall bladders have healing properties. Bears are also often killed to make bear paw soup, which these practitioners consider a delicacy.

The healthiest ecosystems in North Korea came about by accident. Approximately 2.5 miles (4 km) wide, the DMZ between North and South Korea has been left virtually untouched by humans since the 1953 armistice between the two Koreas.[1] What was once an epicenter of military conflict has had a rebirth and is now one of the most valuable nature preserves on the planet.

Stretching 155 miles (250 km) across the peninsula, this no-man's-land crosses wetlands, forests, estuaries, and high mountain ranges. With thousands of landmines still littered throughout the DMZ, it has been described as one of the most dangerous "safe" places in the world. It is unsafe for humans, but a haven for plants and animals. Sixty-seven percent of all the peninsula's plant

The road leading into the DMZ is pictured. North Korea's Diamond Mountains loom in the background.

ENDANGERED SPECIES IN NORTH KOREA

According to the International Union for Conservation of Nature (IUCN), North Korea is home to the following numbers of species that are categorized by the organization as Critically Endangered, Endangered, or Vulnerable:

Mammals	9
Birds	24
Reptiles	1
Amphibians	1
Fishes	13
Mollusks	0
Other Invertebrates	2
Plants	7
Total	57[4]

and animal life can be found in the DMZ.[2] It is home to almost 3,000 plants, more than 300 birds, and approximately 70 different mammals.[3] This pristine patch of land is also home to several endangered species, including the Asiatic black bear and a subspecies of the Siberian tiger, as well as two rare birds, the white-naped and red-crowned cranes.

Development and, strangely enough, peace are the greatest threats to this environmental treasure. In fast-growing South Korea in particular, there is pressure to develop this land; it is naturally beautiful and lies only 30 miles (48 km) from the South Korean capital Seoul. Development has already started to creep nearer to the DMZ. At the Kaesong Industrial Complex, more than 50,000 North Koreans find work producing low-end goods within miles of the accidental nature preserve. On the opposite side of the divide, in Paju, South Korea, only three miles (5 km) away from the DMZ, the population grew from less than 150,000 in 2003 to more than 300,000 in 2008.[5] This development has led to poorer air quality and more river pollution, causing many environmentalists to be concerned that peace between the two Koreas would increase development in the area and thereby threaten species. Others believe cooperation in creating nature conservatories and encouraging eco-tourism might be an important step toward peace.

Animal life typically fares better in the sea than on the land in North Korea. The oceans on either side of the country, as well as the rivers that

GINKGO AND GINSENG

North Korea is one of the few countries in the world where the oldest species of tree is grown, the ginkgo. Its broad leaves are known for their perceived medicinal benefits, and the Chinese have been using the plant for therapeutic purposes for thousands of years. It is also one of the top selling medications in the United States, the United Kingdom, and Germany. It was believed there was only cultivated ginkgo left, but in the late twentieth century some small wild populations of ginkgo were found.

Another plant commonly associated with North Korea is ginseng. The roots and leaves of this herb have been used in traditional Chinese medicine since ancient times. Ginseng has been used to treat many different illnesses and conditions, but its effect on humans is still unclear, and research into its properties continues.

run through it, offer a variety of fish and marine mammals. Types of fish include sardines, mackerel, and yellowtail in the Sea of Japan and Pacific cod, anchovy, and skates in the Yellow Sea. Overfishing in the Yellow Sea has, however, severely depleted stocks. Dolly Varden trout, silverfish, eel, and carp can be found in the rivers. The marine mammals in Korea's seas include an assortment of whale and dolphin species.

FORESTS AND PLANTS

Almost 75 percent of North Korea is forested, with the vast majority of these forests growing on steep mountain slopes.[6] Coniferous trees such as spruce, pine, and Siberian fir are common. In the lowlands, trees such as oak, maple, and ash could once be found in abundance. Deforestation for agricultural purposes has stripped the land of most of them, though, forcing out the wildlife that lived within the forests.

Some reforestation occurred after the Korean War and into the 1990s, as long as North Korea was receiving financial aid from Russia. When the financial aid stopped in the 1990s, however, poverty-stricken North Koreans pillaged the forests for timber and firewood. The lack of forest management has led to river floods, which wash away the rice fields that provide scarce food for the people. It is estimated it would take 4.9 billion trees to reforest the vast barren regions of North Korea.[7]

Sardines are fished in the waters of North Korea.

FLOWERS OF SIGNIFICANCE

The fragrant magnolia is the national flower of North Korea. Two other flowers hold significance for North Koreans. The "Kimilsungia" is a hybrid of an orchid North Korean botanists spent ten years cultivating after Kim Il Sung admired them on a trip to Indonesia; it was presented to Kim Il Sung on his birthday in 1975 and has been common in North Korea since then. Thirteen years later, the manager of the Kamos Iris Garden in Japan developed the "Kimjongilia." This begonia hybrid was presented to Kim Jong Il on his birthday in 1988 and has been called the "immortal flower" or "king flower" since that time.

Diverse plant life can be found in all regions of North Korea. Although it is difficult to collect precise data from the country, it is estimated there are almost 4,000 different species of plants in the country, of which more than 200 are unique to the region.[8] Above the tree line, only alpine plants, including some hardy shrubs and flowers, can survive the cold, harsh weather, but in the warmer southern regions the landscape comes alive with the bright colors of camellias, rhododendrons, and azaleas in the blooming month of July. Mulberry bushes, reeds, and sedges grow along the coastal plains and river valleys where flooding occurs frequently.

The magnolia is the national flower of North Korea.

ENVIRONMENTAL CRISIS

North Korea's environment has been declining since the end of the
Korean War. Many forests were ravaged by fires or cut down for timber

to rebuild the country; even more were cleared for agriculture. In the 1990s, a combination of floods and droughts wiped out rice fields, leaving millions of people without enough food. Once again the forest was stripped for agriculture and fuel.

In 2003, the United Nations Environment Programme published the first ever State of the Environment Report for North Korea. It concluded that in addition to dangerous levels of deforestation, North Korea's water supply was heavily polluted, the air was becoming increasingly polluted, and land degradation was threatening communities and crops with landslides. Things became so bad that in 2012, a North Korean nongovernmental organization known as the Pyongyang International Information Center on New Technology and Economy organized a seminar to learn more about restoring the environment. In a rare move, they invited 13 scientists from countries including the United States, Canada, and China to share information on the subject. The visiting scientists shared conservation techniques used in their home countries. The seminar participants then visited North Korean farms and parks to observe firsthand the environmental problems the country faces. Finally, they discussed future cooperation in tackling these issues.

Damage to the nation's environment can directly impact the well-being of the people.

CHAPTER 4

HISTORY: A LAND OF CONFLICT

The country that we know today as North Korea was created in 1948 after the United States and the Soviet Union agreed to split the Korean Peninsula as part of the Japanese surrender in 1945 ending World War II (1939–1945). For this reason one could argue that its history does not begin until then, and in some ways that is exactly what the current Communist regime wants its people to believe. Except for a few legends and a lot of fanciful tales, North Korean histories tend to begin with the heroic story of Kim Il Sung fighting the Japanese.

CHOSON AND THE THREE KINGDOMS

Artifacts found on the Korean Peninsula indicate people first began to settle there by 6000 BCE. Eventually, tribal groups began to consolidate

Visitors look at ancient Korean artifacts in a museum.

43

power. The most successful of these groups was the Choson kingdom, located in the northern area of the peninsula. Although Korean legend says the Choson kingdom was founded in 2333 BCE, archaeological evidence has dated the kingdom to only 1500 BCE. Artifacts have shown that the Choson people developed iron farm tools and weapons, wooden houses, and chariots. The Choson kingdom was overthrown by the Chinese Han Empire in 108 BCE.

Elsewhere in Korea, during the first century BCE, three distinct rival kingdoms began to take shape: Koguryo, Paekche, and Silla. Many of Korea's cultural and political traditions developed during this period. Similarities can be drawn between these kingdoms and modern-day North Korea.

THE LEGEND OF TANGUN

Korean legend holds that their ancestry began with Tangun. According to the legend, the god Hwanung desperately wanted to live among humans in the mountains and valleys of Earth. His father, Hwanin, granted his son's wish and sent him and 3,000 helpers to Earth. After Hwanung's arrival, a bear and a tiger living in a cave dreamed of becoming human; they prayed to Hwanung, who heard their prayers and offered to grant their wish. He gave each of them 20 cloves of garlic and some mugwort and then ordered them to eat only this and stay out of the sun for 100 days. The tiger gave up after 21 days, but the bear stayed and became a woman. As happy and grateful as she was to be human, she quickly became lonely. Again Hwanung intervened and made her his wife. Soon they had a son, Tangun. Tangun grew up to become a leader. The legend goes that he moved to Pyongyang in 2333 BCE, built his royal palace and capital city, and started the Choson kingdom.

The three kingdoms each grew in size and influence by creating centralized militaries and engaging in war. The kings held incredible power, and their status was passed down to their sons. Tribal chiefs moved from their own communities to the capital and were given the status of aristocrats. The privileges of the aristocrats increased as they advanced to higher positions in society. Higher-class families dominated politics.

Foundation Day, on October 3, is a North Korean holiday that recognizes Tangun.

THE DYNASTIES

The three kingdoms could not live side by side peacefully. More often than not, their conflicts involved China, either as allies or as enemies. After many years of conflict and conquests, Silla conquered Paekche in 660, and in 668 they did the same to Koguryo. This was supported by China at the time. Still, Silla recognized that in order for their people to maintain their independence, they would have to limit the cultural influence of the Chinese Tang Dynasty. By 676, Silla military forces had pushed the Chinese off the peninsula, beginning several generations of Silla rule over the area.

In 935, after nearly 100 years of Silla decline, the region saw a resurgence of Paekche and Koguryo. The general Wang Kon founded the Koryo Dynasty and overthrew the weakened Silla. Wang Kon unified the kingdom on the peninsula, creating for the first time a united Korean kingdom and a singular Korean identity. The people of the area were still heavily influenced by Chinese traditions and cultures. Many students and soldiers traveled to China to study; both Confucianism and Buddhism changed the Koryo Dynasty's style of government. Confucianism, a philosophy based on the teachings of the Chinese philosopher Confucius, emphasized morality, relationships with others, and justice. Buddhism, a religion established in South Asia and which later spread to China, emphasized ethics, meditation, and the desire for freedom from suffering.

Chinese people have been following Confucianism for more than 2,400 years.

The Koryo Dynasty ruled until a military coup in 1170. General Choe Chung Hon led a military regime for the next 60 years. The monarchy no longer held any political power, but its members remained as figureheads.

In 1231, the Mongols, a central Asian empire that had conquered much of the continent, set their sights on Koryo. Their invasion was the beginning of a 30-year struggle that eventually ended with a peace treaty. Though the Mongols annexed some areas of the peninsula into their empire, they agreed they would not control Koryo, and the two empires formed an alliance. In some cases, Koryo kings married Mongol princesses. The Koryo were free to express and maintain their political and cultural identities, but the Mongols did not hesitate to interfere in Korean affairs. They enlisted thousands of Koreans to invade Japan in 1274 and 1281, both times without success.

When the Chinese Ming Dynasty finally defeated the Mongols in 1368, they set the stage for Korea's longest-surviving dynasty, the Choson. The name was borrowed from the Choson kingdom of early Korean history. The Ming claimed control of all Mongol domains in

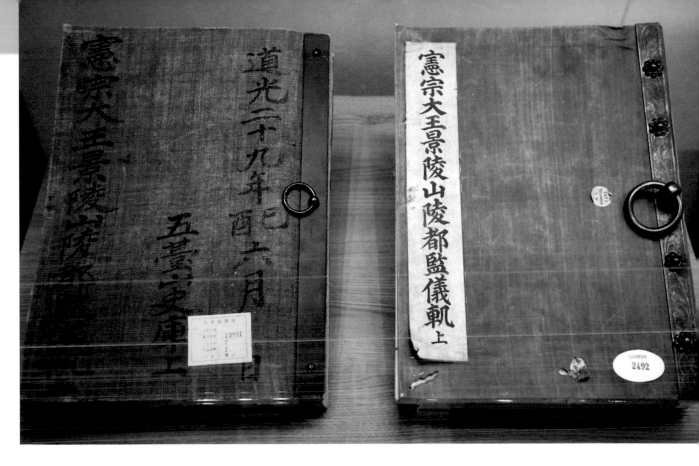

These books of royal protocols date to the Choson Dynasty.

Koryo, which divided the Koryo courts; half were pro-Mongol, half pro-Ming It was the general of a pro-Ming army, Yi Song Ye, who subdued the Koryo capital and became the founder of the Choson Dynasty. He established the capital of Hanyang, which is now the South Korean capital Seoul.

The Choson Dynasty ruled from 1392 to 1910; it was the longest lasting and most successful of all Korean dynasties. The Yi family and its successors redistributed land, increasing the number of aristocrats. The number of scholars grew as well, and the Korean alphabet, Hangul, was created. By the mid-fifteenth century, the Choson Dynasty had established a strong central government and administered eight separate provinces.

Between 1592 and 1627, the peninsula was invaded twice, first by Japan, then by the Manchu of the northeast Asian region of Manchuria. The Choson Dynasty was able to maintain its independence with the help of Chinese forces, but it took decades for the region to recover from the devastation of war. Eventually, investment in irrigation led to better agriculture, and the economy grew to be very strong. In 1876, the Treaty of Kanghwa defined Korea as an independent state and opened diplomatic relations between Korea, Japan, and China.

JAPANESE RULE

As Korea was establishing itself, Japan steadily gained more power in the region. Japan was victorious in both the Sino-Japanese War (1894–1895) with China and the Russo-Japanese War (1904–1905) with Russia. In 1895, China and Japan had signed the Treaty of Shimonoseki, recognizing Korea's independence from China and acknowledging Japan's control over Korean affairs. During the Russo-Japanese War, Korea was forced to allow the Japanese military to use its land for military purposes. Korea was unhappy with Japan's growing dominance, and resistance among the people grew. Believing Queen Min of Korea stood in the way of Japan's ambitions, Japanese agents assassinated her in her own palace in

The funeral procession for
Queen Min

1895. Her husband, King Kojong, remained in power until 1907. His son
then became king, but in 1910 Japan officially annexed Korea, ending the
Choson Dynasty.

Japan ruled the Korean Peninsula from 1910 until the end of World
War II in 1945. Everything Korea did during that time was to serve

Before the war ended, it had already been decided by the allied United States and Soviet Union that Korea would not become independent immediately following the Japanese surrender. It was believed that after so many years of Japanese colonial rule, Korea was not yet ready to self-govern. The United States initially came up with the idea of temporarily splitting the country into northern and southern regions at the 38th parallel, with US forces occupying the south. The Soviets had already taken control of Korean territory in the north in August 1945, during the last weeks of World War II. Although the two nations had been allies during the war, their ideological differences stood in the way of cooperation. Mistrust between the two nations ultimately led to a cold war in Korea.

In September 1945, the Soviet Union introduced Kim Il Sung to the North Korean people. The Soviets were the first to present him as a hero, setting the stage for him to eventually take control of the country as its Communist leader.

Kim Il Sung formed the first central government in February 1946 with his Interim People's Committee. His first course of action was land reforms. Land was taken away from the landlords without compensation and redistributed. In August 1946, several political parties united to form the Korean Workers' Party (KWP). For two years, under the KWP banner, Kim Il Sung amassed more and more power. The South established the independent Republic of Korea on August 15, 1948. A few

Kim Il Sung in 1948

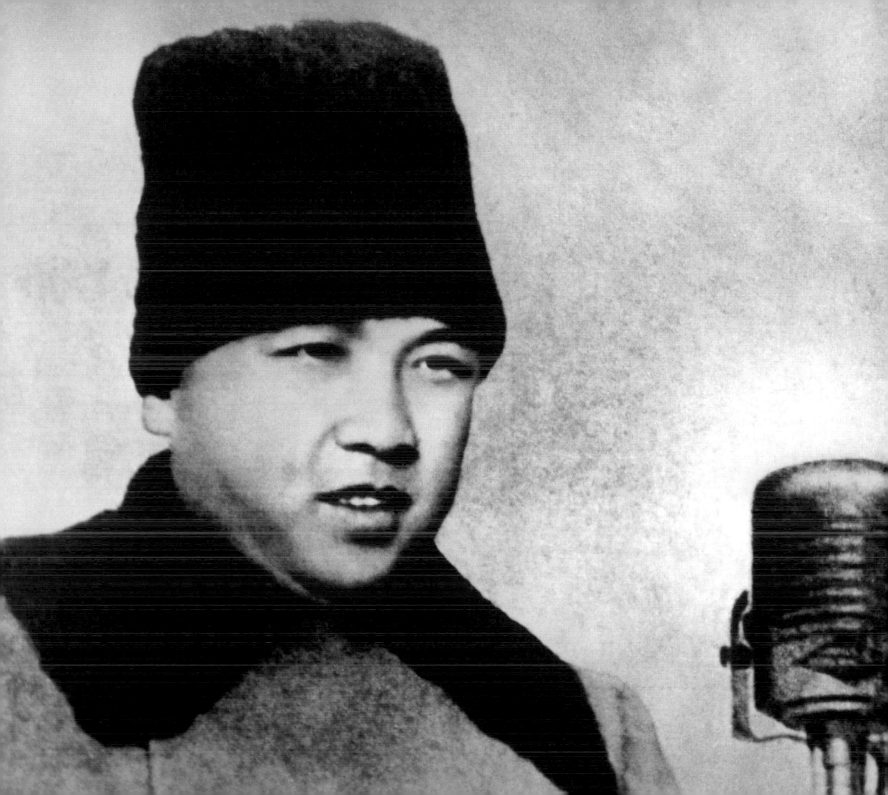

weeks later, on September 9, Kim Il Sung established the North as the Democratic People's Republic of Korea and declared himself its leader.

THE KOREAN WAR

Koreans were angered by the division that was forced upon them; unifying the peninsula became a common political drive for both Koreas. Kim Il Sung in particular used the idea of unification, along with hatred of Americans and Japanese, to gain support from the North Korean people. He rapidly expanded the Korean army and prepared to unify the peninsula under his rule.

By early 1949, Kim Il Sung had fortified the 38th parallel, and he regularly carried out maneuvering drills along the border. Neither the North nor the South recognized the 38th parallel as a real border, and South Korean president Syngman Rhee also talked of uniting the peninsula by force. Small battles started to break out along the 38th parallel on a regular basis, some of them instigated by the South.

Kim Il Sung crossed the 38th parallel with his Korean People's Army (KPA) on June 25, 1950, driving South Korean forces to the southern tip of the peninsula. Having been taken by surprise, the southern forces collapsed quickly. If not for the last-minute intervention of United Nations (UN) forces led by the United States on the side of South Korea, the entire peninsula likely would have fallen to North Korean rule. Along with the UN forces, the South Korean army was able to drive the KPA back across the 38th parallel, all the way to the Yalu River—the

Chinese border. Seeing the rapid advances of the UN troops, Kim Il Sung requested assistance from China's Communist leader, Mao Zedong. Zedong agreed after Soviet leader Joseph Stalin also agreed to contribute air support, and thousands of Chinese troops poured over the border, pushing the South Korean and UN forces out of the North. Two long years of battles without progress or movement ensued. Finally, on July 27, 1953, an armistice was signed. The armistice was only a temporary cease-fire—though there have been no major battles since 1953, the two nations are technically still at war. The demilitarized zone

UN FORCES IN THE KOREAN WAR BY 1953

Republic of Korea	590,911
United States	302,483
United Kingdom	14,198
Canada	6,146
Turkey	5,453
Australia	2,282
Philippines	1,496
New Zealand	1,385
Ethiopia	1,271
Greece	1,263
Thailand	1,204
France	1,119
Columbia	1,068
Belgium	900
South Africa	826
The Netherlands	819
Luxembourg	44[1]

along the 38th parallel was established, and the isolation of North Korea began in earnest.

POSTWAR NORTH KOREA

Kim Il Sung became the country's first president in 1972, and he continued to rule North Korea until his death in 1994. His son Kim Jong Il took over in the middle of a massive food crisis. Unable to continue importing fertilizer from the collapsed Soviet Union, food production fell dramatically. Citizens were urged to eat only two meals per day. Floods in 1995 made the problem worse. Then government officials began hoarding food, and a lack of fuel meant that any food that was available could not be transported. Experts

NAME GAMES

The name for Korea is different depending on where you are from. North Koreans and Koreans living in Russia, China, or Japan call their country Choson after the Choson Dynasty. This is what most consider Korea's original name to be. South Koreans and Korean-Americans sometimes call their home country Hankuk, after the prehistoric tribe first thought to have settled the peninsula. The name Korea itself comes from sixteenth century Portuguese explorers' interpretation of the Chinese pronunciation of Koryo.

The armistice ending the Korean War was signed on July 27, 1953.

Kim Jong Il met with South Korean president Kim Dae Jung in 2000.

estimate up to 3 million people died of starvation during the crisis.[2] The food situation began to improve in the late 1990s, and aid from foreign countries helped bring some stability.

In 1998, newly elected South Korean president Kim Dae Jung enacted what was called the "sunshine policy" toward North Korea. The policy made it easier for South Korean companies to invest in the North and emphasized peaceful coexistence between the two nations, rather than a forceful reunification. The policy led to an unprecedented meeting between Kim Dae Jung and Kim Jong Il in Pyongyang in 2000 and resulted in Kim Dae Jung being awarded the Nobel Peace Prize. However, the relationship between the countries deteriorated after North Korea's 2006 nuclear test. The sunshine policy was brought to an end with the 2008 election of South Korean president Lee Myung Bak, who took a more hardline approach to North Korea.

In late 2011, the food situation once again reached critical levels. It was estimated the country was short approximately two month's worth of food each year.[3] The United States was prepared to send aid on the condition that North Korea halt its long-range missile testing. When North Korea went ahead with an April 2012 launch, the United States withdrew the offer.

CHAPTER 5
PEOPLE: WATCHED AND CONTROLLED

North Koreans are controlled like no other population in the world. Getting to really know the people is virtually impossible, free speech, thought, and expression are all forbidden. What the world usually hears and sees about North Korea is orchestrated by the government, and official government statistics and records cannot always be trusted. But some true stories and facts do escape the country's borders. North Koreans have defected to China and South Korea, leaving their homes and families behind in an attempt to escape the regime. Occasionally a foreign reporter will glimpse something not meant to be seen. The stories of these people provide a rare view of a culture built on propaganda and brainwashing.

North Korean soldiers pose for a photo. Military service is mandatory for North Korean men.

SOCIETAL STRUCTURE

One of the first things Kim Il Sung did after the Korean War was classify every person in North Korea. In order for him to maintain tight control of the population, he thought it necessary to weed out enemies. In 1958, he began his first project, called *songbun*. All citizens were put through background checks to determine their songbun, or rating. These checks considered all aspects of a person's history, including that of their family going back several generations. Loyalty surveys were also regularly distributed.

CLASS DIVISIONS

North Korea's class rating system places people into one of three broad classes. The hostile class includes fortunetellers, shamans, prostitutes, and anyone suspected of being disloyal to the party. These include people who are pro-Japanese or pro-United States, as well as defectors from the South. Those with religious affiliations also fall in the hostile class, including Buddhists and Catholics. The wavering class includes factory workers, farmers, and peasants—those who work hard and sacrifice for the good of the many. Finally the core class includes the military and party members; these are the privileged few that get the honor of living in relative luxury in Pyongyang and other urban centers.

Although equality is the core of the Communist ideal, Kim's goal was to create a class structure that placed him firmly at the top of the social pyramid. Underneath Kim, there were 51 categories that fell within three broad classes: the core class, the wavering class, and the

North Koreans are watched almost constantly by authorities.

hostile class.[1] Where people land in this classification system determines everything about their lives, from where they live and what they do for work to how much compensation they receive to the schools their children go to. Today, a child's songbun is still determined at birth, and it is virtually impossible to move up the class scale.

FAMILY STRUCTURE

Much about the North Korean way of life would seem old-fashioned to an American teenager. As in North Korean society in general, a strict hierarchy exists within households. All family members first honor Kim Il Sung as the fatherly leader, Kim Jong Il as the son of the leader, and recently, Kim Jong Un as the new supreme leader. Then, following the Confucian order, the elderly are revered, and children must show devotion and respect to their parents. Although women and men are theoretically equal in society, women usually prepare all the meals and take full responsibility for raising children, in addition to working jobs of their own. Sons are preferred, as they take over family responsibility from the father.

Many North Korean families were divided after the Korean War. Small communities were merged into larger cooperatives, and the government moved large numbers of people from the countryside to the cities to work in factories; 60 percent of the population now lives in urban centers.[2] Other

KIM'S FAMILY VALUES

In the 1980 article *Kim Il Sung Termed Model for Revering Elders,* Kim's family values are quoted: "Communists love their own parents, wives, children, and their fellow comrades; respect the elderly; live frugal lives; and always maintain a humble mien."[3]

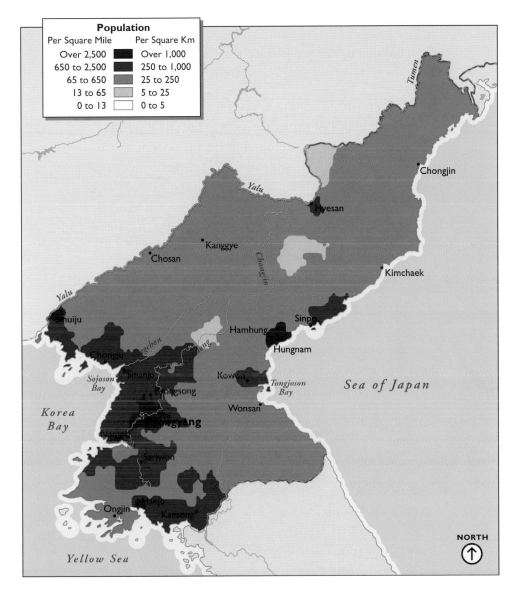

Population Density of North Korea

families were separated by the new border at the 38th parallel, eroding old family ties and cross-country familial networks.

DEMOGRAPHICS

By global standards, North Koreans do not enjoy long life expectancies. The average lifespan is 69 years.[4] Their relatively short lives are the result of poor medical facilities and a lack of medication, combined with ongoing food shortages. Approximately one out of every 400 women dies during childbirth, and one in 40 babies dies at birth. Compared to the rest of the world, this places North Korea near the bottom third in both statistics.[5]

There are no indigenous minorities in North Korea.

There are very few ethnic minorities in North Korea. There is a small population of Chinese and an even smaller group of Japanese wives who married Koreans during the war and returned to the peninsula with their husbands after the war. There were also some marriages between Russians and North Koreans. However, Kim Il Sung launched a campaign in 1963 that encouraged all Koreans to divorce foreign spouses and discouraged future foreign marriages. There is also no diversity in language; all North Koreans speak Korean, and the majority of the world's 70 million people who speak Korean live on the peninsula.[6]

YOU SAY IT!

English	Korean
Hi	Anyonghaseyo (uhn-YOHNG-hah-see-yoh)
Good-bye	Annyonghi gaseyo (uhn-NYOHNG-hee-gah-see-yoh)
Thank you	Kamsahamnida (KAM-sah-ham-nee-dah)
You're welcome	Anieyo (UH-nee-ee-yoh)
How are you?	Chal jinaeshossoyo (CHAL-jeye-nay-shoh-soh-yoh)
Good morning	Annyonghaseyo (uhn-NYOHNG-huh-see-yoh)
Goodnight	Anyonghi jumuseyo (uhn-YOHNG-hee-joo-moo-see-yoh)

RELIGION

Although Korea as a whole was heavily influenced by both Confucianism and Buddhism, most North Koreans now claim no religious affiliation. The 1992 constitution does grant freedom of religious belief, and the government officially acknowledges there are Buddhists, Roman Catholics, and Protestant Christians, but how openly and freely these people practice their religion is difficult to gauge. The closest thing to an official religion in North Korea is Juche.

Juche is the ideology Kim Il Sung used to guide his governance and build his power. Kim defined his ideology as "the independent stance of rejecting dependence on others and of using one's own powers, believing in one's own strength, and displaying the revolutionary spirit of self-reliance."[7] Over time, government propaganda began to present Kim as more of a cult personality. Eventually Juche was adopted as the nation's central principle with Kim Il Sung as its "fatherly leader." Now the only thing most North Koreans worship publicly is Kim Il Sung, his late son Kim Jong Il, and his ruling grandson, Kim Jong Un.

All North Koreans are required to wear a pin bearing the image of Kim Il Sung.

Though North Korea is officially atheist, the Juche ideology is virtually a religion.

CHAPTER 6
CULTURE: A SINGLE THEME

As with most aspects of North Korea, art and culture have been deeply stifled by centralized control. To achieve his nationalistic goals, Kim Il Sung used art and culture as ways to deliver his messages and glorify his ideologies. Today, songs, poetry, books, and paintings are all still created for the government's purposes. The government does, however, promote the teaching of the arts, as long as both the teaching and the creative output of the student are consistent with government ideals. Themes of nationalism and unification are always encouraged. The government is also fond of financing grand displays and celebrations to show off the achievements of North Korea. The grandest of these celebrations is known as the Arirang Games.

The Arch of Triumph in Pyongyang commemorates the victory over Japanese rule.

ARIRANG GAMES

In 2002, in honor of what would have been the ninetieth birthday of the late Kim Il Sung, the first Arirang Mass Gymnastics and Artistic Performances took place in Pyongyang's May Day Stadium. It is now an annual event that involves millions of North Koreans as performers, organizers, and audience members. The show is a display of precise choreography, daring athleticism, and musical excellence.

Gymnasts perform complex routines in perfect unison while children dressed as flowers, fruits, and vegetables dance to promote agriculture and bountiful harvests. In contrast, thousands of soldiers in uniform march onto the field, stopping and posing in timed perfection, while lasers flash and fireworks pop. Perhaps most amazing are the tens of thousands of student audience members who create huge mosaics in the stadium by holding up colored cards at precisely timed points in the performance. But despite the excellence of the performers, the purpose of the show is still clear. Everything about it is orchestrated by the government to promote Korean unity and devotion to the Great and Dear Leaders.

POTTERY AND PAINTING

One of the places where Chinese influence can still be found in Korea is in pottery. In the ninth century, a green-blue pottery called celadon was

Performers at the Arirang Games form the shape of the Korean Peninsula as people in the stadium hold colored cards to create images.

imported from China. For 500 years the Koreans improved production, developing techniques that eventually surpassed those of the Chinese. The intricately designed and delicately painted pottery of this period is often said to be some of the best ever created in Korea. The growth of Buddhism and the related increase in use of teapots led to the production of large amounts of pottery. Lotus blossoms, cranes, and willow trees were common images on teapots.

Historical Korean paintings have much in common with Chinese and Japanese art of the same era. From the Koryo Dynasty up until the beginning of the current Kim regime, landscape painting has been considered the superior art form. A reverence for nature based on Confucian philosophies placed landscapes in a prestigious category. Soaring mountain ranges that inspired awe were a common scene.

After North Korea was formed, art changed. Works of art became propaganda posters for the government. All published artists are state employees who are directed to create work that communicates the correct values and ideals. Paintings and mosaics are very bright, subjects are rosy cheeked, and the sky is always blue. When Kim Il Sung and Kim Jong Il are depicted, they always dominate the scene. Except in the art gallery in Kim Il Sung Square, no other kind of painting is displayed in North Korea.

An anti-US propaganda poster from a Pyongyang kindergarten

MONUMENTS

Large public displays of art are a favorite of the Kim regime. Statues, monuments, mosaics, and towers of immense size can be found throughout the country. Everything on display has to be a little bit bigger or better than anything comparable in the world. The Arch of Triumph that represents the struggle against Japanese occupation is several feet taller than the Arc de Triomphe in Paris. In the village of Kichong-dong, located near the DMZ, stands one of the world's largest flagpoles; at 525 feet (160 m) tall, it supports a 600-pound (270 kg) North Korean flag. On Mansu Hill in Pyongyang stands a 65-foot (20 m) bronze statue of Kim Il Sung. Behind it is a 230-foot (70 m) wide mosaic of Mount Paektu. Just across the Taedong River stands the 558-foot (170 m) Juche Tower.[1] The list of oversized monuments is long, but they all represent the ego of the dictators who ordered their construction more than they do the talent of the artists or the true culture of the North Korean people.

BOOKS AND MOVIES

It is reported that the Grand People's Study House has the capacity to house more than 30 million books. However, North Korea is a heavily censored country, so there is unlikely to be a full selection of Western fiction classics and unbiased nonfiction resources available. Both Kim Il Sung and Kim Jong Il are the authors of countless books, papers, reports,

North Korea's flagpole at Kichong-dong was built in response to a large flagpole built in the DMZ by South Korea.

KIDNAPPED FILM STARS

In 1978, North Korean agents kidnapped Shin Sang Ok and his wife, South Korean actress Choi Eun Hee. Shin was considered to be the father of postwar cinema in South Korea, and Kim Jong Il wanted him to make movies for North Korea. The director and his wife were held in captivity, separately, for four years; neither knew if the other was alive. When they were finally released, Kim Jong Il claimed their imprisonment had been a careless mistake and that they had been brought to the country to improve the movie industry. Shin made seven movies for the North Koreans before he and his wife finally managed to escape in 1986 when they were permitted to travel to Vienna for a business meeting about their next film.

and even songs. When they are not credited as authors themselves, they are featured as heroes fighting the Japanese or Americans, struggling for Korean unity against imperialism.

Movies are yet another medium for government propaganda. Korea Feature Film Studio has produced an assortment of films that tell stories of the great triumphs of Kim Il Sung and the virtues of the Juche ideal. In movie after movie, North Koreans bravely fight and win battles against the Japanese, Americans, and South Koreans. Kim Jong Il even wrote a book about movies, *On the Art of the Cinema*. In it he expressed his belief that the role of movies was to contribute to "people's development into true communists."[2] Occasionally a movie from Russia or China will be played on the four state-run television stations, but in general very little media from the outside world reaches the average North Korean.

MUSIC

Children have a very good chance of getting government-funded musical instruments, so many children are exposed to music at a young age and learn to play an instrument very well. Because it was well regarded by the Dear Leader Kim Jong Il, opera is popular and taking in an operatic performance at the Mansudae Arts or Moranbang theaters in Pyongyang is a treat for the privileged class.

Although radio stations are government owned and censored, North Korea still has its own version of pop music stations. Most of the songs, however, are sentimental, with titles like "Yearning For My Beloved Mother" and "My Home Sweet Home." Some songs are sung by the Korean People's Army Choir, who can also be seen quite frequently on television. Karaoke has become popular in North Korea as well; Frank Sinatra's pop standard "My Way" is a particular favorite.

CELEBRATION TIME

The only holidays during the year, when citizens are allowed to take the day off of work and spend time celebrating and relaxing, are national holidays. It is during these festivities that North Korean women wear the bright traditional costume called the *hanbok*. These colorful outfits with short jackets and long skirts are no longer worn in daily life, but North Koreans who are chosen to perform in national celebrations still wear them.

CHRISTMAS IN NORTH KOREA

For most North Koreans, Christmas is a nonevent. The marketing, pageantry, and religious worship of Christmas simply do not exist in North Korea. Although there are likely several hundred thousand Christians in North Korea and as many as 100,000 practicing in secret churches, generally speaking they do not practice their faith openly or freely. Christians can be arrested for celebrating Christmas, and the persecution and execution of Christian leaders is not uncommon. Despite this, defectors smuggle Christmas gifts to underground worshippers. As one defector said, "Christmas would otherwise be meaningless."[3]

The biggest celebrations in North Korea honor the births of Kim Il Sung and Kim Jong Il. The government puts on displays featuring military parades, fireworks, dancers, and singers. May Day is another big festival; it often includes a performance in the May Day Stadium and the opportunity for a little fun and games for the people.

SPORTS

The Kim family holds athleticism in high regard. Kim Jong Il was reported to be near perfect in a multitude of sports. Although most people did not believe the tales of his multiple holes in one in a single game of golf or of a perfect 300 in his first bowling game at a new alley, these stories do speak to how much he valued athletics.

A massive military parade was held in Kim Il Sung Square in September 2011.

EMBARRASSING LOSS

North Korea entered a soccer team in FIFA's 2010 World Cup for the first time since 1966. After losing a relatively close match to Brazil, the state-controlled television broadcasters decided to televise the team's next match against Portugal. The North Koreans were completely outplayed in what was their third and final game; they lost 7–0 and were eliminated from the tournament. Reports immediately following the loss suggested players were going to be punished for their failure. Rumored punishment included hard labor for the coach and public scolding by more than 400 people for the players. Whether this actually happened is not clear.

The people, however, view their participation in sports as a duty to the leadership. Athletes chosen to perform in the Arirang Games train and practice all year for the event.

In addition to acrobatics of the Arirang gymnasts, athletes participate in traditional sports including taekwondo and wrestling. Western sports including hockey, boxing, and basketball are also played. Soccer is the most popular sport in the country; women's and men's teams compete at the international level. All professional athletes are chosen and controlled by the government, and professional athletes are not idolized the way they are in the United States.

A North Korean soccer player, in red, competes in a 2012 game.

FOOD

Whether on the northern or southern side of the DMZ, the traditional food of Korea is more or less the same. Kimchi is the most popular and common of all Korean dishes. It varies from region to region, but most kimchi includes pickled cabbage or leeks, along with a variety of peppers, spices, and garlic. Traditionally kimchi was jarred in the fall so it would last through the winter. Along with rice it is a staple of most North Korean diets.

Other traditional meals include *bulgogi*, or Korean barbecue, which entails cooking strips of marinated beef on a gas or charcoal grill built into a table. Fish, seafood, and shellfish are eaten often, and similar to the Japanese, North Koreans sometimes eat them raw. *Kujolpan* is a dish for special occasions that consists of a stack of wheat-flour pancakes surrounded by eight different stuffings.

Kimchi is the most popular of all Korean dishes.

CHAPTER 7

POLITICS: ONE MAN, NO VOTES

The political landscape in North Korea is like that of no other country in the world. Since its founding in 1948, the country has been ruled by the Kim family. Though there are many commissions, committees, and ministries, the purpose of all government departments is to affirm the authority of the leader and uphold the Juche ideal of national self-reliance. The government uses propaganda heavily to promote these ideals among the people.

THE CONSTITUTION

North Korea's constitution was adopted in 1948 and has been revised several times since then. It was most recently amended in 2012. In it, the Three Revolutions of Kim Il Sung—Juche ideology, improved

Kim Jong Un observes a military parade in 2012.

technology and economy, and the socialist nationalist culture—are declared as keys to the "complete victory of socialism in the northern half of Korea."[1] When referring to relationships with other countries, the constitution mandates that relationships with friendly countries will be based on "the principles of complete equality, independence, mutual respect, noninterference in each other's internal affairs, and mutual benefit."[2] With regard to the rights of citizens, it provides for free education and medical services for all citizens, and it states that citizens have "freedom of speech, press, assembly, demonstration, and association."[3] Few North Koreans are given the opportunity to speak with foreigners, so it is clear the citizens are not as free as the constitution suggests.

BRANCHES OF GOVERNMENT

Although the totalitarian dictator holds the power in North Korea, there is still a complex government bureaucracy that operates in the country. As in the United States, there are executive, legislative, and judicial branches of government.

The executive branch is headed by a premier, who is assisted by a group of vice premiers and a cabinet. The cabinet includes a few dozen ministers, overseeing such departments as the Ministry of Agriculture, the Ministry of Education, and the Ministry of Culture. The cabinet is responsible for implementing policies but does not play a role in setting them.

The officials in the executive branch are elected or appointed by the Supreme People's Assembly (SPA).

The SPA constitutes the legislative branch of government. It includes 687 members, each elected to five-year terms. All adults are allowed to vote for SPA members. The president of the SPA is technically the head of state, but the dictator actually holds the power. The SPA chooses 15 of its members to make up the SPA Presidium. This smaller group, which meets outside of the regular sessions of the SPA, is responsible for most of the real legislative business.

The judicial branch is led by the Central Court in Pyongyang, and its sole role is to protect the state. Judges are elected to three-year terms by the SPA. Neither legal education nor experience is required

STRUCTURE OF THE GOVERNMENT OF NORTH KOREA

Supreme Leader		
Executive	**Legislative**	**Judicial**
Premier	Supreme People's Assembly (SPA) President of the SPA	Central Court

for appointment. Most legal proceedings are first handled by provincial or special municipal courts and then escalated to the Central Court if necessary. Also included in the judiciary is the Central Procurator's Office. With the help of local prosecutors' offices, this department deals with criminal cases and maintains surveillance over the citizenry.

For local administration purposes, North Korea is split into nine provinces, two province-level municipalities, and two special administrative regions (one for tourism and one for industry). At the provincial level, people's assemblies handle legislative duties and people's committees handle administration. The committees are controlled and operated by the executive branch's cabinet.

The Korean Workers' Party pervades all levels of government in North Korea. The party holds essentially all political power, setting policies and selecting candidates for elections. Although several political parties are supposedly permitted to exist, in reality they are all controlled or sanctioned by the KWP. From the time the Soviet Union put Kim Il Sung in power, the KWP has influenced politics and society through its Communist and Juche ideologies. Party members include workers, peasants, and intellectuals.

On December 17, 2011, Kim Jong Il died, and power was passed down to his youngest son, Kim Jong Un. Unlike his father before him, Kim Jong Un has not spent years moving up the ranks and earning the respect

The funeral procession for Kim Jong Il took place in December 2011.

Kim Jong II, *right,* **and Kim Jong Un,** *center,* **are seen in 2010. Kim Jong Un is now the world's youngest head of state.**

of the government elite. Many believe the top military generals now run the country, and Kim Jong Un is merely a puppet. Others think that because of his Western education, Kim Jong Un might open the country to more capitalism. As of 2012, the government structure remained the same.

PERSONALITY CULTS

North Korea was initially founded as a Communist state, and its first constitution was modeled after the Communist theories of Marx and Lenin. Kim Il Sung stayed particularly true to their teachings regarding central control of resources and production. The constitution states that all means of production are owned by the state. It also makes clear that natural resources, transportation, banks, and all forms of communication are state owned.

PROPAGANDA

Propaganda can be traced back to ancient Greece, when lawyers applied rhetorical techniques to make persuasive arguments on behalf of their clients. Propaganda is essentially the art of spreading information—whether true or untrue—to persuade people. Modern political dictators, such as Nazi Germany's Adolf Hitler, have placed a heavy emphasis on propaganda. As part of his efforts to consolidate power, he formed the Ministry of Public Enlightenment and Propaganda. The role of this department was to ensure that the people of Germany never encountered anything that made the Nazi Party look bad, while at the same time glorifying the regime and its leader. Kim Il Sung followed this model but took it even further. Not only did Kim censor everything and everyone, but he also isolated his country from the rest of the world. He then used propaganda to promote his Juche ideology, his brand of revisionist history, and his right to govern as a deity.

Over time, however, Kim Il Sung started to shift away from the traditional socialist ideal of an egalitarian utopia. His Juche ideology started to take on its own identity, including a belief that it is the state's role to defend nationalism, the nation, and its character. Propaganda

again figured prominently in promoting his new ideals. Juche soon became the sole guiding authority for government. It focuses on North Korea's goals of independence, self-reliance, and self-sufficiency, with Kim Il Sung as the "fatherly leader."

This last aspect forms the center of the North Korean personality cult. The leaders of the country are described in mythical, heroic terms in the country's media. Outside sources have noted that along with the military, the media has been key in keeping the leaders in power. The Kim family appears on billboards, on television, and even on the sides of buildings. When Kim Jong Il was alive, the media continually repeated how selflessly and tirelessly he worked for the

THE KOREAN PEOPLE'S ARMY

North Korea has the fourth largest standing army in the world; only the United States, China, and India surpass it in raw manpower. The Korean People's Army includes more than 1 million active-duty personnel and more than 7 million paramilitary or reserve forces.[4] North Korea's military has approximately twice as many active troops as South Korea. In addition to double the personnel, they possess numerical superiority in tanks and artillery. However, many of North Korea's vehicles and weapons are obsolete Soviet equipment. In contrast, the South Korean military is well equipped, using the latest South Korean and US military technology. The United States has also stationed military personnel in South Korea since 1953 to help them defend against any external aggressors.

Kim Il Sung was declared North Korea's eternal president in 1998.

NO FREEDOM OF DISSENT

When American writer Bradley Martin visited North Korea to research a book, he questioned his guide about the idea of "total unanimity" among the people. Slightly irritated with being forced to answer, his guide responded, "Of course, we have people who dissent; that's why we have police."[5]

benefit of the North Korean people. Every night, the newscast begins with a song about his mythical birth. The same sorts of methods were used to build a cult of personality around his father and are now being used to do so around his son. These cults cannot even be stopped by death. In 1998, Kim Il Sung was declared the country's eternal president.

FAILING SYSTEM

It has become apparent that one of the reasons North Korean leaders keep their citizens so isolated is because they do not want the people to find out the truth about the failures of the regime. The authorities subject the people to daily propaganda about North Korea's superiority, but the reality is much different. North Korea has struggled to support itself for several decades. The country's continued isolation and unstable

The flag of North Korea

political scene make it too much of a risk for international investors. Infrastructure is crumbling. Most of the country goes without electricity for much of the time. Industry and technology have fallen behind, forcing many people to revert to manual methods of doing things. Poor land management and some environmental bad luck have led to an increasingly underfed population. Other countries have sent food aid into the country over the years. However, North Korea's continued military provocations have interrupted this aid and harmed foreign relations.

North Korea is a country with few allies. Since the end of the Korean War, a hatred of Japan, South Korea, and the United States has been built into the national identity. So, too, has military might. After the devastating consequences of World War II and the Korean War, North Korea has made a point of ensuring the world knows they have one of the largest military forces; 20 percent of the country's men serve in the military. The country also continues with nuclear tests despite global appeals for them to stop.

KIM JONG IL'S ARMORED TRAIN

Kim Jong Il, afraid of flying, usually traveled in an armored train. The train was originally given to his father by Joseph Stalin, but has since been updated with luxurious modern features. The regime was paranoid about assassination attempts; residents near a Russian train station he passed in 2011 were reportedly instructed to remain in their homes and not even look out their windows as his train passed. North Korean officials reported that Kim Jong Il died while traveling on his train, though some South Korean sources raised doubts, noting the train had not left the station at the time of death.

The United Nations Human Rights Council has condemned North Korea's human rights abuses. Hundreds of thousands of people the leaders consider politically undesirable are held in prison camps across the country. Former guards and inmates have testified that forced labor, torture, and executions all occur within the walls of these camps. Over the years, many North Koreans seeking escape have managed to defect to South Korea. They have provided much of the information regarding these rights abuses and have deepened the outside world's understanding of North Korea. Some defectors have been threatened by North Korea for their efforts to spread such information.

Historically, North Korea has had strong political ties to both Russia and China. During both World War II and the Korean War, these countries supported North Korea with weaponry and soldiers. After the war, the two countries became North Korea's primary trading partners. However, relations between North Korea and Russia have steadily deteriorated since the fall of the Soviet Union in 1991. And since China has improved its relations with both the United States and South Korea it has had a much more cautious relationship with North Korea. Nevertheless, North Korea still relies heavily on China as a trading partner and for foreign aid, and the countries maintain the Sino-North Korean Mutual Aid and Cooperation Friendship Treaty. Signed in 1961, this agreement pledges that China will render military and other assistance by all means to its North Korean ally against any outside attack. This treaty has been renewed twice, in 1981 and 2001, and remains valid until 2021.

CHAPTER 8

ECONOMICS: A FALTERING SYSTEM

The North Korean economy is a command economy. This means that production and pricing is based on government-set production targets and prices. After the Korean War, the objective of the government was to industrialize the country and drastically increase agricultural output. From the late 1950s into the early 1980s, this appeared to

THE NORTH KOREAN WON

The currency of North Korea is the North Korean won, established in 1947. One won is divided into 100 chon. The currency is only for use by North Koreans; visitors to the country must use either special visitor currency or a reliable foreign currency, such as the euro. In recent decades, North Korea has seen increasing inflation and black-market activity. In 2009, it tried to stop these developments by revaluing its currency. Two zeroes were cut off the end of the currency—100 won was now one won. The change destroyed many North Koreans' savings.

Kim Il Sung appears on one of North Korea's banknotes.

101

work. But the economy eventually began to show signs of slipping; when aid stopped flowing in the 1990s, the downward slide accelerated.

POSTWAR DEVELOPMENT

The end of Japanese occupation in 1945 and the subsequent division of the peninsula was economically devastating for the North. Being cut off from Japan and South Korea denied the North a market for its raw materials and sources of food and other products. North Korea also suffered from a shortage of skilled labor, including scientists, architects, and lawyers, because the occupying Japanese formerly held these positions. On top of all this, there was extensive damage to the country's infrastructure as a result of the Korean War.

CHOLLIMA MOVEMENT

In 1958 Kim Il Sung made an effort to inspire the North Korean people with his Chollima Work Team Movement. Chollima is a mythical winged horse that can leap great distances. Kim used Chollima to represent the "breathless speed of socialist construction and revolutionary spirit of Korea."[1] With a constant eye on increasing productivity, workers were encouraged to excel in the manner of Chollima. Workers were divided into teams, and they competed against each other at increasing production. Although production did increase in some areas during the Chollima movement, other sectors suffered at their expense.

Women work in a Pyongyang textile factory in 2012.

Kim Il Sung set ambitious redevelopment goals. Between 1957 and 1993, he issued a series of economic plans for the country. Varying in length from five to 10 years, the plans set economic goals and production targets. The first few plans were completed ahead of schedule, but starting in the 1970s the country had less and less success achieving its planned goals. In 1993, the government admitted the Seven-Year-Plan running from 1987 to 1993 was not successful. North Korea has not presented an economic plan since then.

North Korea received significant economic benefits from its relationships with China and the Soviet Union. These nations provided military and economic aid, often selling materials to North Korea at "friendship prices." When the Soviet Union and then China reduced their aid and started charging market rates for things such as oil and coal, it devastated the North Korean economy. Reduced fuel imports have led to an unstable power supply in the country, making it nearly impossible to sustain a healthy economy.

In 2009, North Korea's GDP was less than that of North Dakota.

BROKEN NATION

Many problems have stemmed from the country's financial strain. There has been no investment in infrastructure for years; buildings

Trucks bring food across the Chinese border into North Korea.

and equipment are in disrepair, and there is a shortage of parts and tools. Hydroelectric dams that provide over 60 percent of the nation's electricity are out of operation more often than not.[2] Poor farming conditions, including a lack of arable land and a shortage of fertilizer, have added to food shortages. Record-setting floods in 1995 caused severe famine throughout the country, and North Korea has been receiving food aid from international organizations ever since. However, whether North Korean leaders choose to accept aid, where they accept it from, how much they accept, and under what conditions they accept it seems to change on the whim of the leader.

By all accounts, North Koreans desperately need the help. The government of North Korea does not release financial statistics for the country, but there is

FAMINE

The 1990s were not good to North Koreans. A struggling economy meant many of the things required to ensure agricultural output were less available. Production of fertilizer, which is required to grow anything in the country's soil, was reduced. Pieces of farm equipment were breaking down, and there were no spare parts to fix them. When the Soviet Union started charging market prices for oil, North Korea simply ran out of it. The nation's machinery stopped, and crop yields fell drastically. Food shortages became desperate. Irregular droughts and floods further damaged crops, compounding the problem. In 1997, the World Food Programme estimated North Korea required an additional 1.25 million tons (1.13 million metric tons) of food per year to meet the minimum caloric needs of the people.[3] It is estimated that up to 3 million people—10 percent of the total population—died during the famine.[4] North Korea has received foreign food aid since that time.

little doubt it is a very poor nation. Only the privileged few who live in Pyongyang and other cities experience relative comfort. In 2011, it was estimated the per capita gross domestic production (production divided by population) was $1,800, compared to $48,000 for the United States.[5]

One of the biggest barriers to the improvement of North Korea's economy is its lack of foreign trading partners. Currently more than 45 percent of the country's exports go to China and more than 40 percent to South Korea, accounting for most of North Korea's export income.[6] In 2008, the total trade between the two Koreas topped US $1.8 billion, but almost all of it is isolated to the Kaesong Industrial Complex, a special economic development zone set up in agreement with the South Korean government. However, this trade declined dramatically due to heightened military tensions between the nations in 2010.[7]

KAESONG INDUSTRIAL COMPLEX

The Kaesong Industrial Complex, a joint venture between the two Koreas and the South Korean company Hyundai Asan, opened in June 2004. The complex is located in North Korea on the western end of the border with South Korea. Managers who come from South Korea must cross the DMZ to get to work every day. Financed mostly by South Korea, the complex is an experimental economic zone where more than 120 South Korean companies are permitted to operate in North Korea. More than 50,000 North Koreans work at the complex, manufacturing everything from clothing and textiles to kitchen utensils and auto parts.[8]

Most other nations in the world, including the United States, are hesitant to do business with North Korea. When North Korea attacked South Korea in June 1950, the United States placed a ban on trade and commercial activity with North Korea. Over time and through laborious negotiations surrounding North Korea's nuclear program, the United States has started to ease economic sanctions. In 2008, President Bush terminated the Trading with the Enemy Act as it pertained to North Korea, but by 2011 President Obama had issued an executive order prohibiting all imports from North Korea into the United States.

As of 2012, a number of UN sanctions were also in place, a result of North Korea's pursuit of nuclear weapons in violation of UN resolutions. For many years, international observers believed the regime was actively working to build nuclear weapons. This was finally confirmed in October 2006, when North Korea conducted an underground test of a nuclear bomb in North Hamgyong province. In response, the UN passed Security Council Resolution 1718, ordering North Korea to halt its program and banning the export of certain weapons and luxury goods to the country. Another test, this time more powerful, was conducted in the same area in May 2009. UN Security Resolution 1874 condemned this new test, authorized UN member states to search North Korean cargo vessels, and extended the ban on weapons exports. North Korea has also tested long-range rockets that could potentially be used to carry nuclear weapons to faraway targets. A missile test in April 2012, claimed by North Korean authorities to be a

It was reported that North Korea gave China a 20-minute warning before the 2006 test.

A guard stands near North Korea's rocket in preparation for the April 2012 launch. The rocket failed to reach orbit.

In 1998, the two Koreas collaborated on a tourism project that was meant to be a symbolic step toward reunification. Spanning 37 miles (60 km) on Mount Kumgang, Diamond Mountain Resort has an 18-hole golf course, karaoke bars, and hot springs. Located near the DMZ on the east coast of North Korea, the resort received more than 1.9 million South Korean tourists between its opening and 2008.[9] A tourist who was said to be on a restricted beach was shot and killed by Kim Jong Il's troops in 2008. The resort has been closed to South Koreans ever since. In 2012, North Korea approached a US company to reopen the resort and once again attract tourists.

peaceful satellite launch, failed a few minutes after launch.

The fact that many nations refuse to trade with North Korea does not mean it has nothing to offer. Its mountains are rich with natural resources including coal, iron ore, limestone, graphite, copper, zinc, and precious metals. The country has the ability to manufacture artillery, machines, textiles, and chemicals. And if properly managed, North Korean agriculture could produce enough rice, corn, potatoes, and soybeans for its people. Fishing and aquaculture are other areas in which the country could experience growth.

TRANSPORTATION

Another barrier to North Korea's economic growth is transportation. The mountain ranges that crisscross the peninsula make the land difficult to traverse. A struggling economy has meant little money has been put

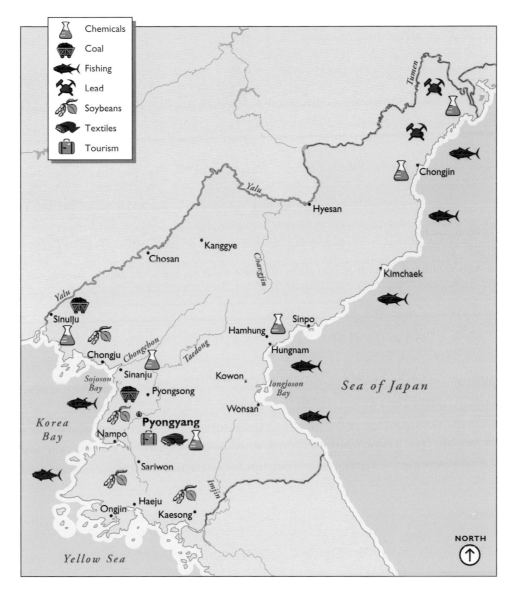

Legend:
- Chemicals
- Coal
- Fishing
- Lead
- Soybeans
- Textiles
- Tourism

Resources of North Korea

into maintaining transportation routes. Ports, railways, and roads all need repairs, upgrades, or expansion.

There are several major ports for moving goods in and out of the country. Nampo on the west coast is the entry port to Pyongyang. Another western port is Haeju. The eastern ports include Wonsan, Hungnam, and Chongjin. But getting goods to and from the ports is a challenge. The main rail routes roughly follow each coastline, with small routes branching off into river valleys, but because of poor maintenance and a shortage of energy sources, the system is not reliable. Motor vehicles are scarce in North Korea, and trucks are not generally used to transport goods. Except for the few major highways connecting Pyongyang to other major cities such as Wonsan, Nampo, and Kaesong, most roads are not paved. The poor infrastructure severely impedes the movement of goods.

POTENTIAL FOR CHANGE

Tourists must have North Korean guides with them at all times.

Visitors contribute to North Korea's small tourism industry. Most come from China, but approximately 500 North Americans visit the country each year.[10] Travel visas are now granted to citizens of the United States and South Korea. The year 2012 marked the one-hundredth anniversary of the birth of Kim Il Sung. North Korea planned many celebrations, including a special Arirang Games. As part of its more open policy, it encouraged foreign visitors to attend.

Even as North Koreans commute to work or school the Kim family watches over them.

In 2002, North Korea embarked on a set of limited economic reforms. The objective was to improve prices, wages, and foreign exchange rates. However, most experts believe the reforms were ultimately unsuccessful. The government did not follow through on the short-lived changes by implementing new policies, and there was no evidence the reforms led to an increase in foreign investment.

CHAPTER 9
NORTH KOREA TODAY

When one looks at a satellite image of East Asia at night, North Korea can be found easily. Most of the nations in the region feature bright clusters of city lights from bustling urban centers such as Tokyo, Seoul, and Beijing. But North Korea is strikingly dark. A tiny spot of brightness marks Pyongyang, but the rest of the landscape sits in total blackness. A shortage of electricity is probably the biggest hardship next to food shortages. Functioning in the dark and living on rations are simply part of everyday life for most North Koreans. The government continues to hold stubbornly to its centralized, military-first style, as well as its nuclear and missile programs. These aims are all pursued at the expense of the well-being of everyday North Koreans.

Kim Jong Il was reported to have owned 17 mansions.

North Korean children line up at a patriotic youth parade. There is little room for individuality in North Korea.

SPYING IS A WAY OF LIFE

Without modern communication systems, it is difficult for the North Korean government to control the population to the extent they do. The only way they are able to achieve the level of control they have is by relying on citizen spies. There are numerous government-mandated spy groups, but most party faithful believe it is the right thing to do to report a neighbor, friend, or family member if they do or say something out of line. Neighborhoods are split into *inminban*, or people's groups. These are groups of approximately 20 families responsible for keeping tabs on each other. Each inminban has an elected leader. The leader reports any inappropriate behavior to authorities. Some defectors have reported that this agency has one informer for every 50 people in the country. There are also youth groups that roam neighborhoods, checking to make sure everyone is wearing his or her Kim Il Sung lapel pin and not violating dress codes. Children are praised for turning in their own parents to authorities for transgressions as small as looking at a photo of the leader the wrong way.

WORK AND LIFE

North Koreans rise early every day, work long hours, often seven days a week, and receive little reward for their efforts. The work they do is determined by their songbun, and their pay is set by the government. The government also provides housing, food, and clothing based on job and geographical location. Compensation usually focuses on providing basic needs first and money second, although this is slowly reversing. City workers tend to fare better than their rural counterparts, and those who live in Pyongyang do the best. Most North

North Korea, outlined here, is almost completely dark compared to the neighboring countries of China, South Korea, and Japan.

Koreans celebrate national holidays; the government permits people to take these days off work. Days of leisure, however, are rare. Time off for vacations is virtually unheard of, and a day at the beach is considered a special treat.

Although maternity leave is allowed in theory, mothers often carry their newborns to work; toddlers typically spend the day in daycare. Children spend little time playing and are expected to put in long hours studying, learning to play instruments, and helping around the house. At the age of 12 they are required to do patriotic volunteer work. Groups of children are gathered together and taken to farmlands to plant rice, weed fields, and spray pesticides.

Approximately 20.6 percent of North Korean children younger than five are underweight.

EDUCATION

The literacy rate in North Korea is very high; 99 percent of adults age 15 or older can read and write.[1] The government began providing free mandatory primary education starting with kindergarten in 1957. Over time, they slowly added the number of mandatory years. Children now attend school for a total of 11 years, including two years of kindergarten, four years of primary school, and five years of middle school. Pupils wear uniforms of navy pants or skirts, white shirts, and red neckerchiefs. There

North Korean schoolchildren perform a dance for foreign visitors.

HUMAN RIGHTS

North Korea has one of the worst human rights records in the world. Torture is commonplace in the labor camps, called *gwalliso*, where political offenders are sent. Collective punishment is also imposed on the extended families of the offenders. And, even with continuing malnutrition among the people, the government continues with its "military first" policy. Freedom of speech, expression, and assembly do not exist.

In March 2012 the United Nations Human Rights Council adopted a resolution condemning human rights violations in North Korea. Julie de Rivero, Geneva director at Human Rights Watch, remarked, "When no state is willing to defend North Korea's record, there can be no doubt that North Korea needs to make real changes."[4]

are more than 6 million children enrolled at these levels of education. North Korea also has 300 colleges and several universities, with close to 2 million students enrolled. Kim Il Sung University in Pyongyang is the only school in the country that offers four-year degrees.

The indoctrination of the young using party ideology begins early. Kim Il Sung explained that the role of education is more than just learning; he noted that it should "train North Koreans to serve the existing social system."[2] One teacher described his role: "We are educating them in the communist morality. We are educating them in a unitary idea—thinking in the same way and acting in the same way."[3]

Boys and girls attend school together until they finish their required 11 years, after which boys usually do their mandatory military service while girls typically work in factories or on farms. Approximately 30 percent of males are exempted from military service and are permitted to continue to high school and then college or university. These young men are usually the sons of high-ranking military or party officials. Acceptance into a university is usually easier after serving in the army; the military chooses which veterans will go on to college and which will be assigned to labor jobs.

There is a shortage of intellectuals in the country. In 1998, Kim Jong Il introduced a system of selecting students to be sent abroad to gain education in the advanced areas of technology and engineering, but the effort made only a small dent in what is becoming a bigger problem. The limited scope of the people's education is yet one more thing that hinders economic development.

INDIVIDUALITY RESTRICTED

Because the government provides everyone's basic needs, individuals do not tend to express themselves through their clothes, homes, or hobbies. Citizens must adhere to strict dress codes, and even hair length is monitored. Although North Koreans do sometimes wear Western styles of clothing, many wear uniforms on a daily basis, and coworkers usually dress the same. Dress is also often a good indication of a person's position or class; army and paramilitary uniforms are always khaki, police uniforms are black, and members of the navy wear blue and white.

SIX PARTY TALKS

In August 2003, the Six Party Talks began among the United States, Russia, China, Japan, South Korea, and North Korea. The objective was to convince North Korea to end its nuclear weapons programs. The talks have faltered from the beginning, suffering long periods of delay. In 2009, North Korea quit the process. A short time later, it revealed a new uranium enrichment facility and tested a second nuclear weapon.

In February 2012, Kim Jong Un announced that the country would suspend its nuclear program and allow International Atomic Energy Agency (IAEA) inspectors to verify activity at the uranium enrichment facility in exchange for food aid from the United States. But in April, after the North attempted to launch a satellite that the observers believed was simply an excuse to test long-range missiles with the potential to carry nuclear warheads, the United States suspended its promise of food aid. The rocket's failure came at a huge cost to North Koreans. In addition to the loss of promised food aid, the rocket also cost US $450 million to build.

A man wearing a suit made from lightweight fabric from Japan would likely hold an upper-class position, as would children wearing foreign-made clothes.

Housing also lacks personality. Most North Koreans outside of urban areas live in what are called harmonica houses. These are very long rows of homes that are open on the side where all the entrances are located. The design makes the building look like a harmonica. Each home is approximately 100 square feet (9 sq m) and has a kitchen and one room. It is nearly impossible to tell one home from the next. The same can be said for the large apartment blocks city dwellers live in.

LIFE OF A TEEN

Teenagers in North Korea do not have, nor does it appear they expect, the freedom teenagers from most Western nations have. Their daily lives are monitored, scheduled, and planned from birth, and even their own parents have little to do with the direction their children's lives take. They honor their parents and elders and work hard for the good of the community with little question. Computers, the Internet, and popular music are not part of their everyday lives. They do not own cell phones, and the authorities do not permit the idolizing of movie stars or athletes.

A defector spoke about dating in North Korea: "It took us three years to hold hands. Another six to kiss."

Teens generally do not date; physical contact between members of the opposite sex who are not married is prohibited. And socializing with someone outside a person's class hierarchy could have a negative impact on his or her future.

Entertainment is found in simple pleasures. Walking in the park, staring at the stars at night, and talking about books or movies are all common pastimes for the young. For more daring youngsters, the constant darkness from power failures creates opportunities for secret meetings with friends after the adults have gone to bed for the night. But in general, the younger generations are stronger believers in the Kim regime than are the older generations, who still have memories of Korea before it was divided.

FUTURE OUTLOOK

North Korea's future is difficult to predict. World leaders, international organizations, and nonprofit organizations around the world agree the country's situation is perilous. There is a willingness to help, but everyone expects North Korea to make concessions if it wants help. Putting an end to its nuclear program would be a major step toward gaining international support, and improving human rights and opening its borders to more foreign influence would also help bring North Korea into the twenty-first century.

Little is known about "the great successor." Since assuming power in late 2011, Kim Jong Un has done little to convince people he has any plans to change course from his father's leadership. For now, it looks as though

NOTHING TO ENVY

In her book about North Korea, *Nothing to Envy*, author Barbara Demick described an unsettling sight: "For lack of chairs or benches, the people sit for hours on their haunches, along the sides of the roads, in parks, in the market. They stare straight ahead as though they are waiting—for a tram, maybe, or a passing car? A friend or relative? Maybe they are waiting for nothing in particular, just waiting for something to change."[5]

Little is known about Kim Jong Un, the leader of North Korea since December 2011.

the people have accepted their new leader, but how long this will last is another uncertainty.

They might not express it, but North Koreans are apparently aware their government is failing them. A coal miner from Chongjin explained their reaction this way, "People are not stupid. Everybody thinks our own government is to blame for our terrible situation. We all know we think that and we all know that everybody else thinks that. We don't need to talk about it."[6]

Though North Koreans are aware of how dire their situation is, it may be difficult or impossible to change it.

TIMELINE

6000 BCE	People settle on the Korean Peninsula.
1500 BCE	The Choson kingdom is established.
First century BCE	Silla, Koguryo, and Paekche consolidate their power on the Korean Peninsula.
676 CE	Silla military forces push the Chinese off the peninsula.
935	Wang Kon founds the Koryo Dynasty.
1231	Mongolia invades Koryo. After conquering the peninsula, they use it as a base to launch two failed invasions of Japan.
1392	Yi Song Gye establishes the Choson Dynasty. Under the Yi family reign, Choson was the longest lasting Korean dynasty.
1592	The Korean Peninsula is invaded by Japan.
1627	The Korean Peninsula is invaded by the Manchu.
1876	The Treaty of Kanghwa defines Korea as an independent state.
1904	Russo-Japanese War begins; Russia ultimately loses, giving Japan control of the Korean Peninsula.
1910	Japan annexes the Korean Peninsula, controlling it until the end of World War II.

1945	The United States and the Soviet Union divide Korea at the 38th parallel; the US controls the South and the Soviets control the North.
1946	In August, several political parties unite to form the Korean Workers' Party (KWP).
1948	In August, the South establishes the Republic of Korea.
1948	In September, Kim Il Sung establishes the Democratic People's Republic of Korea (DPRK) and the first constitution is adopted.
1950	On June 25, Kim Il Sung crosses the 30th parallel and invades the ROK..
1953	On July 27, an armistice temporarily ceases the military conflict of the Korean War.
1994	On July 8, Kim Il Sung dies, putting his son Kim Jong Il in power.
1998	The constitution is revised to acknowledge Kim Il Sung as the eternal president.
2000	Kim Jong Il meets with South Korean president Kim Dae Jung in Pyongyang.
2006	On October 9, North Korea tests its first nuclear weapon, resulting in UN sanctions.
2009	On May 25, North Korea tests its second nuclear weapon, resulting in additional UN sanctions.
2011	On December 19, Kim Jong Il dies of a heart attack; his youngest son, Kim Jong Un, is named the "great successor."

FACTS AT YOUR FINGERTIPS

GEOGRAPHY

Official name: Democratic People's Republic of Korea (DPRK)

Area: 46,540 square miles (120,538 sq km)

Climate: Generally consistent and mild climate. The rainiest months are June through September. Winter months can get extremely cold in the northern interior.

Highest elevation: Mount Paektu, 9,000 feet (2,744 m) above sea level

Lowest elevation: Sea of Japan, 0 feet (0 m) below sea level

Significant geographic features: Several high mountain ranges with long, deep, narrow river valleys geographically divide the country. The coastline is uneven and relatively long.

PEOPLE

Population (July 2012 est.): 24,589,122

Most populous city: Pyongyang, 3,000,000

Ethnic groups: Almost 100 percent Korean. There is a small Chinese community and an even smaller group of Japanese wives.

Percentage of residents living in urban areas: 60 percent

Life expectancy: 69.2 years at birth (world rank: 151)

Language(s): Korean

Religion(s): There is no official religion, and over 60 percent of Koreans say they have no religion. Most North Koreans worship the Kim family.

GOVERNMENT AND ECONOMY

Government: Communist state; one-man dictatorship

Capital: Pyongyang

Date of adoption of current constitution: 1948; most recently amended in 2012

Head of state: dictator

Head of government: premier

Legislature: Supreme People's Assembly

Currency: North Korean won

Industries and natural resources: military products, machine building, electrical power, chemicals, mining (coal, iron ore, limestone, graphite, copper, zinc, lead, and precious metals), metallurgy, textiles

FACTS AT YOUR FINGERTIPS CONTINUED

NATIONAL SYMBOLS

Holidays: February 16, Kim Jong Il's birthday; April 15, Kim Il Sung's birthday; May 1, May Day; August 15, Liberation Day; September 9, Founding of North Korea

Flag: Three horizontal bands of blue (top), red (triple width), and blue; the red band is edged in white; on the hoist side of the red band is a white disk with a red five-pointed star.

National anthem: "Aegukka" or "Ach'imun pinnara"

National animal: None, though the national symbol is a mythical winged horse named Chollima

KEY PEOPLE

Kim Il Sung (1912–1994) took control of North Korea in 1948 and ruled until his death in July 1994.

Kim Jong Il (1941–2011), the son of Kim Il Sung, led North Korea from 1994 until December 2011.

Kim Jong Un (1983 or 1984–), Kim Jong Il's youngest son, rose to power after his father's death in December 2011.

PROVINCES AND MUNICIPALITIES OF NORTH KOREA

Province; Capital

Chagang; Kanggye

North Hamgyong; Chongjin

South Hamgyong; Hamhung

North Hwanghae; Sariwon

South Hwanghae; Haeju

Kangwon; Wonsan

North Pyongan; Sinuiju

South Pyongan; Pyongsong

Yanggang; Hyesan

Municipalities

Rason

Pyongyang

GLOSSARY

arable
Suitable for farming.

armistice
A temporary truce between warring parties.

Buddhism
A religion that originated in India and then moved to China, Japan, and Southeast Asia.

bureaucracy
A term used to describe the unelected administrators within a government's bureaus and departments.

communism
A system of social organization based on communal ownership of all property and resources and central control of the economy.

Confucianism
A system of ethics taught by Confucius that stresses education, reverence for elders, and love for humanity.

conifer
Trees producing seeds in cone form.

Demilitarized Zone (DMZ)
A stretch of no-man's-land that runs along the 38th parallel between North and South Korea.

guerrilla fighters
Usually small, irregular military forces that use nontraditional, surprise methods of attack on their enemy.

homogenous

Of common origin.

Juche

The North Korean ideology founded by Kim Il Sung that guides all government directions and decisions.

monsoon

A very strong wind that changes directions with the seasons.

nationalist

A person who is devoted to his or her nation and who advocates or fights for its independence.

peninsula

An area of land completely surrounded by water except for the small strip of land attaching it to the mainland.

propaganda

The distribution of information that supports or glorifies the doctrine or ideals of the distributor.

typhoon

A tropical cyclone or hurricane that occurs in the western Pacific Ocean.

ADDITIONAL RESOURCES

SELECTED BIBLIOGRAPHY

Demick, Barbara. *Nothing to Envy: Ordinary Lives in North Korea.* New York: Spiegel & Grau, 2010. Print.

Harris, Mark E. *Inside North Korea.* San Francisco: Chronicle Books LLC, 2007. Print.

Hoare, James. *Culture Smart! Korea.* London: Kuperard, 2005. Print.

Willoughby, Robert. *North Korea.* Guilford, CT: Globe Pequot, 2003. Print.

FURTHER READINGS

Gifford, Clive. *North Korea.* Tarrytown: Marshall Cavendish, 2010. Print.

Heather, David. *North Korean Posters.* New York: Prestel, 2008. Print.

Kim, Hyejin. *Jia: A Novel of North Korea.* San Francisco: Cleis, 2007. Print.

Salter, Christopher L., Gritzner, Charles F. *North Korea: Modern World Nations.* New York: Facts on File, 2007. Print.

WEB LINKS

To learn more about North Korea, visit ABDO Publishing Company online at **www.abdopublishing.com**. Web sites about North Korea are featured on our Book Links page. These links are routinely monitored and updated to provide the most current information available.

PLACES TO VISIT

If you are ever in North Korea, consider checking out these important and interesting sites!

The Demilitarized Zone (DMZ)

The DMZ between North and South Korea is one of the most fascinating places on Earth. Almost all agencies that operate tours of North Korea offer tours to the DMZ.

Grand People's Study House

Located in Kim Il Sung Square on Namsan Hill, the Grand People's Study House has the capacity to hold 30 million books.

Kim Il Sung Square

Located in the heart of the capital city Pyongyang, this is also where you will find the Grand People's Study House.

Korean Central History Museum

Located in Pyongyang, this museum displays relics and remains from ancient history to modern times.

SOURCE NOTES

CHAPTER I. A VISIT TO NORTH KOREA

1. "DPR Korea 2008 Population Census National Report." *Central Bureau of Statistics, DPR Korea.* United Nations Statistics Division, 2009. Web. 8 Aug. 2012.

2. "In Pictures: Vast Crowds at Kim Jong-Il Memorial." *BBC News Asia.* BBC News, 29 Dec. 2011. Web. 8 Aug. 2012.

3. "Pyongyang Educational Establishments." *Juche Travel Services.* Juche Travel Services, n.d. Web. 8 Aug. 2012.

4. "Pyongyang Monuments and Architecture." *Comtourist: Eastern Bloc Travel, News, History and Media.* Comtourist.com, 2010. Web. 8 Aug. 2012.

5. "North Korean Leader Kim Jong Il Dies 'Of Heart Attack'" *BBC News Asia.* BBC News, 19 Dec. 2011. Web. 8 Aug. 2012.

6. Mark E. Harris. *Inside North Korea.* San Francisco: Chronicle Books, 2007. Foreword. Print.

CHAPTER 2. GEOGRAPHY: MOUNTAINS, VALLEYS, AND SEAS

1. Eric C. F. Bird. *Encyclopedia of the World's Coastal Landforms.* New York: Springer, 2010. *Google Book Search.* Web. 31 Aug. 2012.

2. "The World Factbook: North Korea." *Central Intelligence Agency.* Central Intelligence Agency, 31 July 2012. Web. 8 Aug. 2012.

3. "Sea of Japan." *Encyclopædia Britannica.* Encyclopædia Britannica, 2012. Web. 8 Aug. 2012.

4. "Korea Bay." *Encyclopædia Britannica.* Encyclopædia Britannica, 2012. Web. 8 Aug. 2012.

5. "The World Factbook: North Korea." *Central Intelligence Agency.* Central Intelligence Agency, 31 July 2012. Web. 8 Aug. 2012.

6. "Kaema Highlands." *Encyclopædia Britannica.* Encyclopædia Britannica, 2012. Web. 8 Aug. 2012.

7. "North Korea." *Encyclopædia Britannica.* Encyclopædia Britannica, 2012. Web. 8 Aug. 2012.

8. "The World Factbook: North Korea." *Central Intelligence Agency.* Central Intelligence Agency, 31 July 2012. Web. 8 Aug. 2012.

9. "North Korea." *Encyclopædia Britannica.* Encyclopædia Britannica, 2012. Web. 8 Aug. 2012.

10. "North Korea." *Weatherbase.* Weatherbase, 2012. Web. 2 Aug. 2012.

CHAPTER 3. ANIMALS AND NATURE: THE ACCIDENTAL PRESERVE

1. "The World Factbook: North Korea." *Central Intelligence Agency*. Central Intelligence Agency, 31 July 2012. Web. 8 Aug. 2012.

2. Tony Azios. "Korean Demilitarized Zone Now a Wildlife Haven." *Christian Science Monitor*. Christian Science Monitor. 21 November 2008. Web. 8 Aug. 2012.

3. Mary E. Connor. *The Koreas*. ABC-CLIO: Santa Barbara, 2009. 4. Print.

4. "Summary Statistics: Summaries by Country, Table 5, Threatened Species in Each Country." *IUCN Red List of Threatened Species*. International Union for Conservation of Nature and Natural Resources, 2011. Web. 2 Aug. 2012.

5. Tony Azios. "Korean Demilitarized Zone Now a Wildlife Haven." *Christian Science Monitor*. Christian Science Monitor. 21 Nov. 2008. Web. 8 Aug. 2012.

6. Bhang Hyeong Nam. "Severe Deforestation in N. Korea." *Dong-A Ilbo*. Donga.com, 26 Nov. 2011. Web. 8 Aug. 2012.

7. Ken Piddington. "DPR Korea: State of the Environment." *United Nations Development Programme*. United Nations Development Programme, 2003. Web. 8 Aug. 2012.

8. John Hudson. "The Environment Is So Bad in North Korea They'll Even Let Americans Help." *Atlantic*. Atlantic Wire, 3 Apr. 2012. Web. 8 Aug. 2012.

CHAPTER 4. HISTORY: A LAND OF CONFLICT

1. Ed Evanhoe. "United Nations Command. Troop Strengths." *The Korean War*. The Korean War. 22 July 2011. Web. 8 Aug. 2012.

2. "'3.5 m North Koreans Starved to Death.'" *BBC World: Asia-Pacific*. BBC News, 30 Aug. 1999. Web. 8 Aug. 2012.

3. Tania Branigan. "North Koreans Will Die From Malnutrition Within Months." *Guardian*. Guardian. 21 Dec. 2011. Web. 8 Aug. 2012.

CHAPTER 5. PEOPLE: WATCHED AND CONTROLLED

1. Doug Bandow. "Songbun Communism." *American Spectator*. American Spectator, 19 June 2012. Web. 8 Aug. 2012.

2. Robert L. Worden. *A Country Study: North Korea*. Library of Congress, 2008. Print.

SOURCE NOTES CONTINUED

3. "The World Factbook: North Korea." *Central Intelligence Agency*. Central Intelligence Agency, 31 July 2012. Web. 8 Aug. 2012.

4. Ibid.

5. Ibid.

6. James Hoare. *Culture Smart! Korea*. Kuperard: London, 2005. Print. 150.

7. Robert L. Worden. *A Country Study: North Korea*. Library of Congress, 2008. Print. 204.

CHAPTER 6. CULTURE: A SINGLE THEME

1. Mark E. Harris. *Inside North Korea*. San Francisco: Chronicle, 2007. Print. 27.

2. Ibid.

3. Geoffrey Cain. "How Christmas is (Not) Celebrated in North Korea." *TIME*. TIME World, 24 Dec. 2009. Web. 8 Aug. 2012.

CHAPTER 7. POLITICS: ONE MAN, NO VOTES

1. Robert L. Worden. *A Country Study: North Korea*. Library of Congress, 2008. Print. 204.

2. Ibid. 195.

3. Ibid. 195.

4. Ibid. xxvi.

5. Bradley K. Martin. *Under the Loving Care of the Fatherly Leader*. New York: St. Martin's, 2006. Print. 6.

CHAPTER 8. ECONOMICS: A FALTERING SYSTEM

1. Bradley K. Martin. *Under the Loving Care of the Fatherly Leader*. New York: St. Martin's, 2006. Print. 102.

2. Marty Matlock. "Water Profile of North Korea". *Encyclopedia of Earth*. Encyclopedia of Earth, 21 Oct. 2008. Web. 8 Aug. 2012.

3. "Special Report: FAO/WFP Crop and Food Supply Assessment Mission to the Democratic People's Republic of Korea." *World Food Programme*. World Food Programme, 25 Nov. 1997. Web. 8 Aug. 2012.

4. "'3.5m North Koreans Starved to Death.'" *BBC World: Asia-Pacific.* BBC News, 30 Aug. 1999. Web. 8 Aug. 2012.

5. "The World Factbook: North Korea." *Central Intelligence Agency.* Central Intelligence Agency, 31 July 2012. Web. 8 Aug. 2012.

6. Ibid.

7. "Background Note: North Korea." *US Department of State.* US Department of State, 12 Apr. 2012. Web. 8 Aug. 2012.

8. Eric Martin and Sangwon Yoon. "North Korea Recruits New Yorkers to Revive Resort Where Troops Shot Guest." *Bloomberg.* Bloomberg News, 9 Feb. 2012. Web. 8 Aug. 2012.

9. Ibid.

CHAPTER 9. NORTH KOREA TODAY

1. "The World Factbook: North Korea." *Central Intelligence Agency.* Central Intelligence Agency, 31 July 2012. Web. 8 Aug. 2012.

2. Robert L. Worden. *A Country Study: North Korea.* Library of Congress. 2008. Print. 122.

3. Ibid.

4. "UN Human Rights Council: North Korea Condemnation Goes Unopposed." *Human Rights Watch.* Human Rights Watch, 23 Mar. 2012. 8 Aug. 2012.

5. Barbara Demick. *Nothing to Envy: Ordinary Lives in North Korea.* New York: Spiegel & Grau, 2010. Print. 294.

6. Ibid.

INDEX

agriculture, 24, 37, 41, 44, 48, 50, 72, 101, 106, 110, 118

animals, 31–32, 34–35, 37

area, 19–20

Arirang Games, 71–72, 82, 112

art, 71, 74, 77

artifacts, 43–44

bordering countries, 20

Buddhism, 46, 67, 74

cell phones, 8, 123

Chaeryong River, 23

China, 8, 20, 21, 23, 32, 41, 48, 50, 55, 57, 61, 74, 78, 95, 99, 105, 107, 122

Choe Chung-hon, 46

Chongchon River, 23

Chongjin, 28, 112, 126

Choson Dynasty, 46–49, 57

Choson kingdom, 43–44

climate, 24, 27

Cold War, 51

communism, 10, 13, 20, 21, 51, 55, 62, 64, 78, 93, 120

Confucianism, 46, 50, 64, 67, 74

constitution, 13, 67, 87–88, 93

currency, 101

demilitarized zone, 10, 20, 31–32, 34–35, 55, 77, 107, 110

earthquakes, 24

education, 50, 88, 120–121

endangered species, 34

environmental threats, 31, 34–35, 37, 39, 41

ethnic groups, 14, 50, 66

exports, 107–108

families, 64, 66

famine, 106

fishing, 21, 37, 110

flowers, 38

food, 84

foreign relations, 48, 59, 88, 98–99

forests, 32, 37–38

government structure, 88–89, 91–92

gross domestic product, 107

Haeju, 27, 112

Hamhung, 28

Han Empire, 44

Hangul, 48

holidays, 79–80

housing, 116, 122

human rights, 99, 120, 125

immigrants, 66

imports, 74, 105, 108

independence, 54

industries, 107, 110, 112

Japan, 16, 21, 24, 46, 48–50, 62, 66, 74, 77, 78, 84, 98, 102, 122

Juche ideology, 16, 69, 78, 87, 91, 93, 95

Kaema Highlands, 23

Kangnam range, 23

Kim Dae Jung, 59

Kim Il Sung, 11, 13, 14, 16, 20, 21, 38, 43, 50–52, 54–55, 57, 62, 64, 69, 72, 77–78, 80, 93, 95–96, 102

Kim Il Sung Square, 10–11, 16, 74

Kim Jong Il, 10, 13, 21, 38, 57, 59, 64, 69, 74, 77–80, 91, 95–96, 98, 110, 121

Kim Jong Un, 13, 64, 69, 92, 122, 125–126

Koguryo, 44–45

Korea Bay, 20–21, 23

Korean Peninsula, 13, 16, 19, 23, 27, 31, 43, 49, 51

Korean People's Army, 54, 79, 95

Korean War, 14, 16, 37, 39, 54–55, 62, 64, 98–99, 101–102

Korean Workers' Party, 52, 91

Koryo Dynasty, 45–46, 74

Lake Chonji, 21, 24
leaders, current, 13, 64, 92, 125–126
Lee Myung Bak, 59
life expectancy, 66
literature, 77–78

Manchuria, 48, 50
Mao Zedong, 55
media, 14, 78, 95–96
Ming Dynasty, 46
Mongols, 46–47
monuments, 77
Mount Paektu, 21, 24, 77
mountains, 19–21, 23, 27, 32, 110
music, 79, 123
Myohyang range, 23

Nangnim Mountains, 23
natural resources, 93, 110
nuclear weapons program, 108, 122

official name, 13–14, 17

Pacific Ocean, 24
Paekche, 44–45
painting, 71, 74
personality cult, 95–96
plants, 32, 34–35, 37–38
political parties, 52, 91
pollution, 35, 41

population, 16, 17, 24, 66
pottery, 74
poverty, 37, 106
precipitation, 27
propaganda, 16, 20, 21, 61, 69, 74, 78, 87, 93, 96
Pyongyang, 7–8, 10, 17, 20, 24, 27–28, 44, 59, 62, 72, 77, 79, 89, 112, 115–116, 120

Queen Min, 48

Rason, 28
religion, 17, 46, 67, 69
rivers, 23–24, 35
Russia, 8, 20, 32, 37, 48, 51, 57, 66, 78, 98, 99, 122

Sea of Japan, 19–21, 23, 37
Seoul, 34, 47, 115
Silla, 44–45
Sinuiju, 28
social classes, 45, 51, 62–63, 121, 123
South Korea, 14, 20, 23, 24, 34, 35, 47, 54–55, 57, 59, 61, 78, 95, 98–99, 102, 107, 110, 112, 122
Soviet Union, 43, 51, 52, 57, 91, 99, 105, 106
sports, 80, 82
Stalin, Joseph, 55, 98

Taebaek Mountains, 23
Taedong River, 10, 23, 77
Tang Dynasty, 45
Tangun, 44
teenage life, 123
38th parallel, 20, 52, 54, 57, 66
tourism, 35, 91, 110, 112
trade, 107–108, 110
transportation, 8, 93, 110, 112
Treaty of Kanghwa, 48
tsunamis, 24
Tumen River, 20, 23
typhoons, 24, 27

uniforms, 118, 121
United Nations, 41, 54–55, 99, 120
United States, 16, 41, 43, 50, 51, 52, 54, 59, 82, 88, 95, 98–99, 107, 108, 112, 122

volcanoes, 21, 23, 24

Wonsan, 27, 112
World War II, 16, 21, 43, 49, 50–52, 98–99

Yalu River, 20, 23, 54
Yellow Sea, 19, 20, 37
Yi Song Ye, 47

PHOTO CREDITS

Maxim Tupikov/Shutterstock Images, cover, 2, 5(top), 15, 25, 29, 30, 60, 114, 129 (bottom); iStockphoto, 5 (center and bottom), 12, 63, 68, 70, 76, 100, 131; Claudia Dewald/iStockphoto, 6; Matt Kania/Map Hero, Inc., 9, 22, 26, 65, 111; Liu Zaoming/AP Images, 18; Ken Brown/ iStockphoto, 33, 128; Rich Carey/Shutterstock Images, 36; Tatiana Brzozowska/iStockphoto, 39, 130; Harvey Meston/Getty Images, 40; Kyodo/AP Images, 42, 47; Frank and Francis Carpenter Collection/Library of Congress, 49; AP Images, 53, 56, 58; Elizabeth Dalziel/AP Images, 73; Ng Han Guan/AP Images, 75, 127; Kyodo News/AP Images, 81; Binod Joshi/AP Images, 83; Shutterstock Images, 85; Korean Central News Agency via Korea News Service/AP Images, 86, 90, 92, 94; Paul Cowan/Shutterstock Images, 97, 132; Pedro Ugarte/Getty Images, 103; Anu Nousiainen/Getty Images, 104; Pedro Ugarte/Getty Images, 109; David Guttenfelder/AP Images, 113; NASA, 117; Ian Timberlake/Getty Images, 119; KNS/AFP/Getty Images, 124